GOGGLES

FOR | INNOVATORS, ENTREPRENEURS, RESEARCHERS

GOGGLES

FOR
INNOVATORS,
ENTREPRENEURS,
RESEARCHERS

BY

SUDHANSHU MAURYA

White Falcon
Publishing

www.whitefalconpublishing.com

Goggles for Innovators, Entrepreneurs, Researchers
Sudhanshu Maurya

www.whitefalconpublishing.com

ISBN - 978-1-947293-42-7

Preface

In today's times, innovation is taking place at lightning speed, in each and every aspect of our life. These are challenging times for traditional processes to innovate things in which you work quite hard to accumulate knowledge and later, you come to know about your goal of life. It is time to look over challenges and meet the technology to solve them so as to get excitement, happiness, satisfaction and joy whatever the goal of life is. This book is not the sole source to provide to everything to start innovating, but a book that can help you a little to make the right move.

The book contains information about solving the problems of the world with the help of science. It does not require someone out-of-the-world to solve the problems but people like you who combine their experience, assumptions, beliefs, excitement, madness, hard work derived by fear and imaginations and beat the odds to come out with solutions that can change the world.

You have to serve people and get money in return. You either serve others by working with them or do something which itself help others. You have two ways of solving the real life problems. You may either go with the traditional formula where you continuously get good grades in examinations. Quite later in life, you may identify certain topics with the help of your study, which is quite uncertain; if you are lucky enough in choosing the topic and your working formula.

Or you may get involved in finding the problems and solving them with enhanced mind-set or bullet proof formula that can be found in this book and come out with a solution by beating the odds. The problem which you work upon may turn into philosophy, invention, innovation, business, product, process, etc.

Contents

"Ok, now, come with me and remember, the person you are going to meet is our boss, the business head of this whole yarn plant. So choose your words wisely and I'll try my best to get the project passed," my project guide assured. His words helped, only to escalate my already pounding heart. I nodded like an obedient child. "Where are your project details?" he asked as if I was the sloppiest person on earth. Meekly, I raised my file and said, "It's all here".

It was not about the completion of the project or the benefits to the plant associated with it. For me, it was the money which I'd get if my training project was passed.

"Ok, give it to me, and follow me," he said.

"Yes sir," I complied and handed over the file to him.

Throughout the whole spinning around of the last two months, for the project with him, my project guide was never much humble to me, but today seemed to be the worst of all days.

Within seconds we were in front of the business head. His busy face dug into a notepad he was scribbling something in, and his agitated expressions immediately emanated the vibes I dreaded the most - rejection. He didn't seem to be in a good mood either.

"Sir, this is Rajendra, the intern I talked to you about this morning, for the training project review," my project guide broke the awkward silence. The business head paused his pen and looked up.

"Oh, yes yes. Have a seat," he pointed to the empty chairs in front, removing his spectacles.

"Hmm... So you are Rajendra," he said as we took our seats.

"What are the topics for your projects then?" he asked.

"Sir, the first one is about the reduction of breakage rate from 1.5 to 0; and the second one pertains to increasing the moisture regain percentage in cotton yarn from 1.5 to 2.25, at Xorella," I replied.

"And what's your solution to attain these tremendous numbers?" he asked. Was he mocking me? I had put in immense efforts to bring about the project details in a file, in the best possible way, only for this man, and he seemed least interested even to glance through it. It was demotivating. I really wanted to say, 'look at the data given here. It's much more impressive than the actual solution.' But I ended up explaining myself.

"Sir, for the breakage reduction in Simplex, I found that the major cause of breakage is fhutki – the entangled mass of fibers, mostly seen as fragments. Another substantial reason is the breakage in the neighboring bobbins. These causes are triggered because the RSBs are not cleaned properly, introducing impurities into the mixture and causing the breakage at Simplex. In another project, I found that the major cause of moisture escaping the package was the delay in packaging. Hence the overall moisture level was low."

"Did you ask the operators about it?" he asked.

"Yes sir, I did," I replied.

"Do you understand the drawbacks of packaging the yarn bundle early?" the business head asked.

"Yes sir, it actually condenses on the polyethene of the package and is known as a fault because it may create patches on the package and invite bacteria," I answered.

"Did you try the post-conditioning process?" he did not stop.

"Yes sir," I replied, trying to take the heat positively.

"What were the outcomes and why you didn't prefer that?" I seemed to be in the firing line.

"Actually, sir, when we put the packages in post-conditioning, the temperature of the room rises steadily and that's why it has no significant moisture retention effect," I tried to convince him.

"What was the temperature after rising?" he asked.

2

I replied, "It would be nearly 50 degree Celsius. It's too hot for anyone to sustain in there."

"It's not possible. Do you know what happens at that temperature? Did you measure the temperature?" he asked as if he knew the answer already, which I guess he did.

"No sir, I did not," I answered, a little ashamed.

"Oh! You didn't even measure the temperature and you are predicting things on that," he laughed sarcastically.

I felt embarrassed. By what means could I tell him, being an intern, how difficult it was to get one's hands on any equipment, even as small as a thermometer?

He looked at the clock. It was lunch time. Still in his own thoughts, he got up and started walking towards the canteen. We followed him.

"When you go to a doctor, does he give a medicine by just touching your hand?" he scolded.

"No sir," I replied, looking at the floor.

"Go on then, get the post-conditioning temperature reading and then come back to me," he said and left us stranded in the middle of nowhere. It just sounded like 'Get lost'.

I came to the processing plant again and somehow managed to get a thermometer. I measured the temperature and found it to be 41 degree Celsius. 9 degrees lower than what I had quoted. The reading dashed my hopes of getting the project signed. Now I could just hope he would have calmed down by the time I meet him again. I had to face him again, this time not with my project guide, but with my foolishness. Post lunch, with nervousness gripping me all over, I entered his cabin again, to collect my share of insults.

"Sir, the temperature was about 41 degree Celsius," I said.

"You were saying it to be 50? What happened to the remaining 9 degrees?" he was proud of winning this argument and proving that I was worthless. But he didn't stop, "And you are suggesting that the packing of the bundle at the right time is the solution? Anybody could give this suggestion. You are from an engineering college, and I'd expect some good technical

3

solution from your side. You didn't suggest any change to the Xorella machine," he ended.

Please, someone tell him how difficult it is to make a change in any machine, that too when you don't even know its working principle.

No doubt I made a mistake, but I had put in a lot of effort, so I gathered some courage and asked, "Sir, is my report not worth anything?"

"I didn't look inside, but your topic is fine. Where do I sign?" He raised his pen, uninterestedly. That moment gave me some relief. All the insults were worth it then!

"You are from which college?" he asked.

"Sir, the Government College of Textile," I replied with a sigh of relief.

But it was not over yet, "That's a good college, but how do they induct students like you? Have they stopped taking entrance exams?"

I was numb. Already unsatisfied with myself, and with all these offenses, I thought I didn't even deserve this college now, a college which was not even on my top list. Like everyone else, I have strengths and weaknesses. I don't know how good my strengths are, but I do have a heavy load of weak points. These weak characteristics of mine are so weak that even the below average students can easily surpass me in them. That was the reason, even being a good, diligent student why I started going downwards. I don't mind being lonely, but I hardly fit in with most of my colleagues.

I returned to my college, but the whole training process had made me even more concerned about my future. On one side were my passions - getting innovative ideas, working on them, doing research work, knowing more about scientists, innovators, knowing how anyone got those eureka moments in innovation, while on the other side there was this calculated conventional path experienced by others – jobs.

Living most of my early life alone and having a curious mind, I strayed into reading scientific books and magazines. These had a major role in inculcating the interest of innovations in me. My thinking wandered into various fields. My focus, unlike most people around me, was innovations, irrespective of the field. Being engaged to one field for a long time, gaining expertise in that, I started dreaming of a new arena. My colleagues thought it was very difficult, especially because we were not experts at that.

Most of the students of my college would go for jobs. Some would pursue higher education and then go for jobs, while many others would push themselves to get into government jobs. So, I had two paths – one, following my passion, and the other, the one followed by most people, getting a job.

The path of passions was surely an uncertain one. On it, I appeared to be a child with birth defects who wanted to live but was not strong enough. My dilemma of following the passion or getting a job always made me weak. At one moment, on each little success, I would connect the dots, tracing a beautiful future where everything was clear, while the next moment, the moment of failure, everything was scattered and the dots just did not connect, again the dilemma overpowering me. While the moments of success are motivating, enjoyable, and fun, the moments of failure are annoying, pushing you down. There are times when you meet people who are experts at something. And you realize you are pretty much nothing, just another amateur. I gave a lot of time to these thoughts. I was enjoying my life somehow, but these thoughts held the key to my future.

After returning to the college I started going to a nearby park for morning walks. As it was very close to the college, and hardly any students are interested in getting up early, the park remained almost empty in the morning, although some elder people did come here. But this was the only place near my college which was devoid of students, early morning. I felt really good getting up early. By the time fellow students got up, it seemed, I was already half a day ahead.

One morning I woke up very worried. I did not know why, but the previous night I had these thoughts which made me quite tense. I guess, whenever I think a lot before sleeping,

I wake up much perplexed the next morning. Somehow, I got out of the bed and went to the park. I did not walk; I just sat on a bench. There were the usual elder people walking around, but this day, I also saw a young man taking rounds on the ground. He looked smart and fit, pretty different from the others present there. Soon, probably finishing his final round, he came to my bench and sat next to me. He turned on his mobile and opened an app. I couldn't help but glance and saw the app was YourStory. I had recently installed it on my phone and was very impressed with their articles and information.

"Do you read the articles on YourStory regularly?" I asked.

"Yes, they are very well updated and provide some good, useful information," he replied.

"Did you read the article on Ritesh Aggrawal, the founder of OYO Rooms?" I inquired. "Oh yes! That was a good story, and inspirational too, especially for you guys. Are you from the nearby textile college?" he questioned. I nodded. "And, did you install the YourStory app recently?" he asked. "Yes! How did you know?" my voice rising with surprise and excitement. "Only those who are new to it show such curiosity," he stated. I felt a little self-conscious. "But how did you know about my college?" I quizzed.

"I just guessed," he said, and his phone rang. He picked up the call and started talking to someone. Sitting right next to him I couldn't avoid overhearing the conversation about some innovation and patent. This person seemed worth the meet. I was much aware of the term innovation as I had read a few books on that, like Innovators Dilemma, Innovation, and Entrepreneurship by Peter F. Drucker. But the word patent, I had heard it before, but not researched it yet.

He cut the phone call and resumed the talk with me, "So, what's your name?"

"Rajendra, and you?"

"Robin. Ok Rajendra, I need to go now. Nice to meet you," he said.

"Same here," I responded, and then he left.

* * *

The next morning I came to the park a little early. I had hardly met people with such knowledge, and I hoped he would come again. I had some questions for him.

I just walked around the park for some time and sat on the same bench. Soon enough, he also came, greeted me and sat on the bench.

"Are you waiting for your girlfriend?" he asked.

"No. I am just sitting here because I got up early and had nothing better to do. Why did you think that?" I asked out of curiosity.

"Looked like it. But seems you are not satisfied with your life," he replied.

"That's somewhat true. Are you an astrologer?" I asked.

"No."

"Then what makes you think so?" I interrogated.

"I'm just wondering if the activities for engineering students have been changed or they are the same as before," he chuckled.

Now seemed to be a good time to ask the questions I had, "Can you tell me something about innovation?"

"Yes sure. But before that, could you tell me more about yourself?" he asked. A bit unprepared, I replied, "I'm in the third year of my graduation in the textile stream. Research, innovations, startups, and business interest me a lot," I was just going on when he interrupted, "You have interests in business, start-up, research, and innovations! Do you have any experience in these?"

"I have some idea about them, and just a few months ago I won a competition in my field where I had pitched an innovative idea and won a prize. Besides, I've also won the first prize in entrepreneurship in the college competition," I added continuing, "Although I have won various prizes, I lack confidence. I have reached a point where I think I am not a master of this field. Many questions come to my mind which leave me speechless. And as I am always battling with myself how can I compete with others? Well, that's about me. Would you like to know anything specific?" I checked.

He just waited for some time and then spoke, "quite interesting. Yes, something important and similar to others."

"Is this astrology?" I asked again, but he just grinned and didn't respond. He remained silent for some time. He wasn't ignoring me but seemed to be thinking something seriously. Little did I know, those thoughts were going to play a big role in my life.

He explained certain things to me then and said he was going out of town for about a week and would talk to me more once back. He left me to ponder over the thoughts, and soon I got engaged in college days again.

What he told me changed my life completely. It even changed the way I looked at things - products, processes, etc., the way I undertook my studies, the way I found problems and their solutions, the way I thought about the society, science, and almost everything around. Basically, my outlook towards various things got a whole new direction. Initially, I tried to apply it to just a few things, but slowly, I was able to apply such a thought process to almost everything.

Not only my outlook and attitude changed, but I was also able to differentiate between the attitude and thinking of the various professors at college.

One professor used to tell me to work hard, get into any better college for post-graduation, and secure my future with a job. He regarded the undergraduates as incompetent and unsuitable to contribute much towards the innovations or real life problems. He considered these problems to be much more complex than our abilities to solve them and wanted us to focus on the projects which had been already completed successfully by other students before us, presenting us how they did it, making us followers. He used to ask us to consider improving what was already there, and always told to learn and then do things. Working with him was like finding the faults and correcting them. No doubt he was a technical expert, and not that his advice was always wrong, but it was not the best, at least for a person with a curious and creative mind like me.

Another professor, who was much more experienced and practical than the first one, told me to focus on the topics, the solutions to the problems I wanted to solve, and named them as 'A' (I'll just come to this in a moment). He inspired me to attempt solving bigger problems, even when I was just an undergraduate, and wanted me to focus on those topics which were lesser taken up by other students, due to high complexity. Unlike the first professor, he taught me to learn by doing. He explained the working of our mind and made us understand how this knowledge would help us perform much better in life. He taught me to focus on my strengths and made me mentally strong. Having gained the required strength even before starting a project, and working on it with a clear and focused mind, helped me get rid of the faults and obstacles.

But before I tell you more about myself and what happened with me later, let's talk about 'A'. 'A' can be looked at or represented in many ways. In case you find it hard to understand the concept of 'A', you may simply think of it as an 'idea', although it's much more than that. Please see the diagrammatic representation of how 'A' links the various things easily. Finding a solution for 'A' for the terms on the left could lead to any of the outcomes listed on the right-hand side of the diagram. Say, a problem may not be called an idea, but a problem may lead to an idea. 'A' can be looked upon as a 'topic' of interest, on which you wish to work on.

Once you decide a topic, say windmills, you could arrive at an idea, a problem statement, a new way of using them etc. Working on which could lead you to invent something new, or innovate something, maybe start a whole new business, and could lead to a betterment of life.

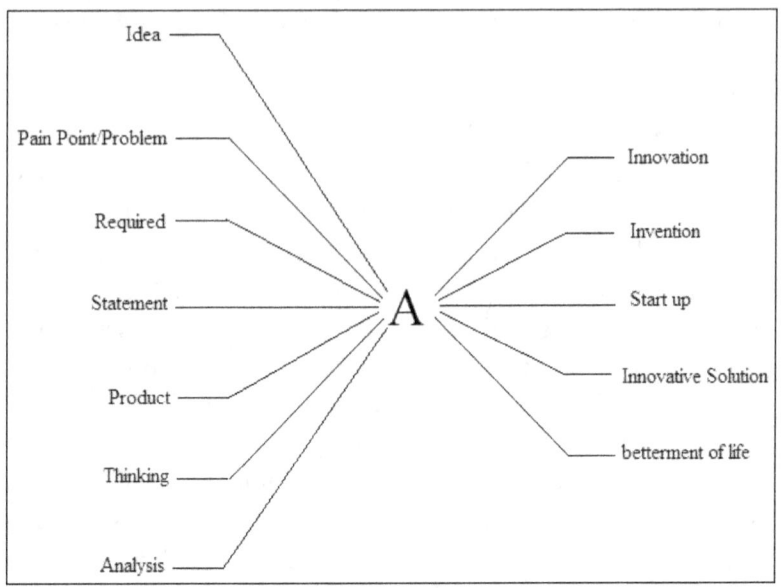

On the left-hand side, we have a starting point or a possibility of 'A', while the right-hand side lists the possible results of working on 'A'. In short, if we're working on an 'A', we'd finally want a solution or an answer to it which could lead to any one or more on the right-hand side of the diagram.

I met Robin many times after that and the next section covers how those meetings unraveled things for me.

Section-1

Myth:
Have lots of knowledge then have 'A'

"You need to remove some of the traps laid down by your mind or put into you by others. Everyone has some filters, and they can hinder your progress," he said when we met after his week-long trip.

"I'm sorry, but I'm not sure about these traps and filters. Could you explain these to me in detail?" I said, sounding a little confused.

The kind man explained - whenever you are unable to digest some points, means you have a filter which screens the information and affects your understanding. This filter could be right or wrong. Like, whenever someone says that only hard work alone can get you success, you stumble, because from your experience you know that it's not just the hard work but also the smart work that is required to achieve success. You have a filter from your personal experience.

These filters may also be called retarders, opposite forces or mind distracters.

"What are you good at?" he asked.

"I think, public speaking," I replied.

"What do you notice when your colleague says that he/she can't speak in public?"

I said, "Probably they are thinking too much about what people think about them."

He continued explaining, "In the same way when you start innovating something or getting the solution to 'A', many things come to your mind, and some may require being removed, else you may never accomplish your goals. These things are known as retarders or the negative filters which slow you down and may even push you to leave aside 'A'. You have to be smart enough to identify them and beat them before they can beat you."

He pointed out that there are two types of retarders:

1. Common retarder.
2. Specific retarder.

The common retarders are those which occur to most people when they are trying to do something for the first time, especially while thinking about innovations. For example, "is there anything left to innovate?" "Innovations require lots of knowledge." "There are people smarter than me." "I am don't even feel like reading even a single page, how can I finish the whole book?"

These are common retarders which come to most people when they try their hands on something for the first time. Analyzing historical data, and taking examples from many experienced people, we know that most of these are false feelings. Still, every time we are not able to beat these, sometimes we lose.

"Ok, and what are specific retarders?" I asked.

"Tell me an idea which came to your mind and you thought you are going to invent something," he asked.

"A mechanism, which could be installed in shoes, and could convert the mechanical energy of walking into electrical energy," I replied.

"What happened to that idea?" he asked.

"I stopped working on it as I felt I do not have much knowledge and potential to work on it," I replied.

He said that he won't comment on my discarded idea but enquired, "May I ask why you did not pursue the problem and try to get a solution to it? Is it that you are a textile engineer and you can do well only in that field?"

"I think getting a solution to this requires lots of knowledge. If I could get more knowledge first, then I could work on it, and maybe, I am able to find a solution to it with much ease," I replied.

"You are like a foolish engineering student who will always have a scarcity of knowledge. You may have a Ph.D. on your crush but you will never have the knowledge which is going to make her your future," he said teasingly.

He continued, "The problem is, this attitude and thinking are not only found in common people, but also in the renowned teachers and professors who teach you. What they say is not entirely incorrect, but it's how they put it to you folks, the young minds, that matters. It may definitely require some good amount of studying, research, and a reading of many books, but these educators sound like – those who are involved in innovations must have read a lot many books, and should have done quite a lot of research before working on an innovation, and they cannot be involved with anything else. In 1980's, even the experienced people would say that establishing a business was tough, innovating things was tough, doing research was a big task. If we look at it today, even the younger generation is contributing towards innovations. Earlier, only some countries had the capability to innovate things, but today, every small country is giving its contribution towards innovations and inventions."

He paused, like he just remembered an anecdote, "While pursuing matriculation, my physics teacher would say 'beta ye physics hai, bahut mehnat karni padegi ise seekhne ke lie' (Son, this is physics. You'll need to work a lot harder to comprehend and absorb it)."

15

Robin explained, if you ask the definition of 'a lot', it may differ from person to person:

1. Some may say it's about gaining many skills.
2. Some may say it's about reading ten or hundred or even more number of books.
3. Some may say it's about reading abundant books and putting plentiful time in research after graduation (some may refer it after post-graduation).

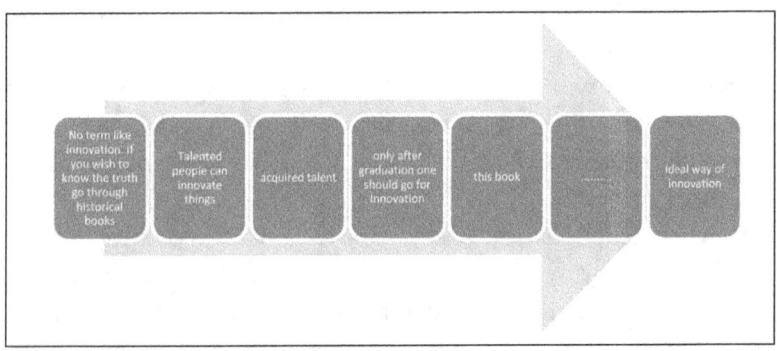

The arrow shows a timeline of how the perception of innovation moved.

In the ancient times, say even before the likes of great minds like Newton, whenever people wanted some knowledge they were asked to go through the historical books. Innovations or any new findings were not easily or well accepted, especially if they contradicted the knowledge already etched in old books. Ordinary people were meant to be followers and were not expected to do something useful for mankind. Each and everything had been done already by a God or their ancestors.

After that, the term 'talent' came down to play a role. Although people with talents were very few, as most were following the old conventions, some people shined with talents or skills in some areas of life and were able to solve and logically answer some of the riddles of those times. Many concept related innovations, inventions, and answers originated in this age. Some started monetizing the ideas while some helped in social service.

Slowly, we moved to an age, our current one, where we have training centers like colleges, universities, etc. so that we can acquire specific skills, based on our interests and try to contribute towards innovations and inventions through our attained talents and skills.

Although we may be yet to reach the ideal way to innovations, we may be close now.

Primary knowledge is that which is required to arrive at a research topic ('A') and to work on the elementary things, i.e. the basics. **Secondary knowledge** pertains more to the specifics of working in detail. For example, if you are going to work on a solar concentrator ('A' = wanting to work on solar concentrator) then you should have the primary knowledge about the surface reflector, as well as about the phenomenon of light. So to say, how you chose this topic to work upon, how you arrived at this topic, your 'A', you need some primary knowledge.

Now, practically, to work upon 'A' you would be required to know these things in detail. Secondary knowledge is all about the specifics and details. It's like gaining expertise and can be acquired by anyone with primary knowledge. Let's take an example - a person can be a doctor with the primary knowledge, and he/she decides to work further on the heart ('A' = want to work further on the organ 'heart'). Now, to be a heart specialist, he/she needs the secondary knowledge, specific to the heart. This knowledge will come over and above the basic primary knowledge, he/she gained while becoming a doctor. Gaining secondary knowledge is like gaining an expertise in a specific area.

"Can you please give me an example where someone very young has done something remarkable?" I asked.

"Yes, why not," he said. "A 15-year-old boy, Jack Andraka, invented a way to detect pancreatic cancer. His detection method is quite simple, low cost, and faster than many complex modern techniques. At this young age, he did not have much knowledge about biology, when he started working on his idea. But by the time he found a solution he was an expert at it. He just followed the rules of innovation instead of following the common view that you should enter the arena of innovations and inventions only after graduation. Let me give you another example. Two girls discovered a way of degrading phthalic acid, a major ingredient in polyethene. They were basically working on degrading the plastic waste but accidentally came out with a bacteria which can easily degrade phthalic acid, which in turn helps in the degradation of plastic. These girls put many scientists, as well as the conventional thinking behind them."

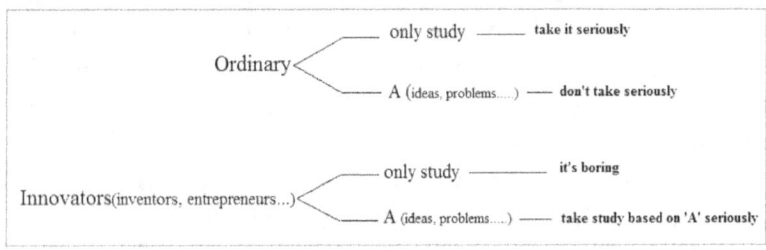

He continued, "Stop saying 'when I have lots of knowledge, when I have graduated, when I have read a lot of books, I will start getting at 'A' and its solution'. Don't stop yourself. Go and search for more examples which show that age is no barrier to innovate. In the above chart, you may find many of your colleagues in the 'ordinary' section. They may do much better in other areas, but in innovation, you will definitely be the better one. It would be wiser if you decide your 'A' and then gather as much knowledge required around it, rather than simply sitting and waiting to finish gathering all the knowledge and then deciding your 'A' – the topic or topics you would want to work upon, where you would want to solve some real life problems and might come up with some innovations or inventions."

Myth:
High education means more probability to get appropriate 'A' and its solution

"You say you are interested in research and innovation and want to find solutions to some real life problems?" he asked.

"Yes, very much. I do," I replied.

"So what do you do about them, how far do you go to achieve them?" he asked.

"I read quite a lot and many times am up the whole night thinking about them," I said.

He continued, "That's good, but not enough. If you don't grow your interest fast enough you may become quite unproductive. And if your source of income is also going to be through this, then the matter gets more serious. In such a case you have to incubate your interest, else all you will get will be a failed experience or an unproductive self."

"Can you tell me more about this?" I asked.

"When I was a kid I was very fond of playing cricket. I used to play a lot. Just like me, I guess, many of your friends would also have had a very keen interest in cricket, but it may not be active now. As I grew, I went to a city, 25 km away from home, for further studies. Over the weekends, I used to come home and play cricket with my friends. Whenever I did not get a chance to play, maybe due to exams or other commitments, I would miss it a lot. I had very few friends where I went to study, and hardly got any time to play when I was there. Soon, as time passed, after around two years or so, I found that I was no longer a good player. I wanted to play more, but it was just not possible. As more time passed, I found that I had even lost my interest in playing cricket. Now, whenever I tried to play, I had a very poor performance. Thus I don't play cricket anymore. In fact, I don't even say that I have an interest in playing cricket.

Nowadays, many students show interest in start-ups and innovations. Like you, there have been many students who had interests in research and invention. But slowly, as their interests went unproductive, maybe because they kept waiting to graduate, new responsibilities of being independent came over them, their interests got lost, and they were not great at those things anymore. There is a pressure to decide about what to do in future. Unable to think clearly, failing to give a chance to their interests at the right time, they start getting depressed. Soon, all they care about is getting placed somehow, and earn some money from their jobs. When they go for the job, everything changes. With the everyday work, on things that may not interest them as much, they realize that they have missed an opportunity to follow their interests and have entered the wrong lane. So now, they advise others to follow their passions, their interests, and not lose the opportunity to do wonders.

In the same way, to stay in the correct lane, you need to know and be aware of the major breakthroughs that are taking place in your time, the real life problems that come in your way as the time passes. Keep your senses open, and be prepared for these," he said.

"There is one thing I don't understand. When I go for higher studies I will have more knowledge, then shouldn't I start searching for my topic of interest then, rather than now? Maybe, an idea that comes right now makes a fool out of me," I asked.

"It is better to make mistakes in practice than in war," he said.

"Most people think that only experts in any subject have the possibility to innovate anything. They are mostly influenced by Edison, Graham Bell, Tesla, Newton, APJ Abdul Kalam etc. These are the people who have done something very remarkable and thus are known to everyone.

People think you should have at least a post-graduate or a doctorate to start thinking about innovations. It all starts with a perception that if a person has more knowledge (let's name knowledge as 'B') then he/she must have the capability to innovate on 'A'. Also, when we attain the required 'B', we think that people who have already the same 'B' would have already thought of that, which again leads us to not work on 'A'.

It cannot be assured that doing Ph.D. will be helpful to attain that 'something else' you are looking for. In fact, there could be a possibility that you could have had it at an early age, and you may probably not be able to have it at a later stage. If you've not explored yourself before the age of 25, there is good chance that a higher age will only increase your fear and lessen the chances of getting that 'something else'.

If you are a Ph.D. holder, it means you are an expert in one of those countless topics. So if you are asked to start working on something else, you'll be the same as others.

Undergraduate + practiced on a few ideas + have read some books could be better than normal Ph.D.

Once you have your topic ready as an undergraduate, you will have four years to explore that. Then, if you need a Ph.D., it will not only be very helpful but also more meaningful for your work," he paused.

"If having more 'B' meant having more 'A' and its solutions, then your professors and seniors would have the most possibility to have an 'A' and its solution. This is just a hypothesis. Do you think that fat people can run longer than a healthy person in spite of having more energy condensed in their body?" he asked.

"I think what you are saying is right. Had that been correct, the major breakthroughs would have been possible only by professors, seniors, or toppers. If I am curious enough, attentive to the problems, and have an ability to solve them, I may turn out to be a good business person with an innovative business or a researcher with renowned papers. But tell me, how will I get the ability to solve 'A' or the obstacles I face while working on it, being an average student?" I asked with excitement.

"Have patience, you will be ready for them when the time comes," he replied.

Myth:
There is a lack of opportunity

"I don't think there are enough opportunities to chase. I mean, for the last one week I brainstormed a lot; I did get a few ideas but I guess many people already have those and are working on them. Hence, most of what I think gets thrown away, and I have started to wonder if there are enough opportunities left to chase now," I said.

"Oh! You just gave me a good opportunity by saying so," he said with a smile.

"Opportunity? I can't find one for myself, how did 'I' give you one? I don't get it?" I wondered.

"You say, you don't have enough opportunities to chase. Now, I know many peoples who have many ideas, but they are already engaged in some of them, or maybe, do not have the time or resources to pursue them, owing to their jobs or other responsibilities. If I could connect this with a business or an innovation, things could flow smoothly and quickly. By doing so, the students will have no lack of ideas and the people having ideas will be satisfied that some work is being carried out in pursuit of their idea," he said.

"But isn't it happening already? I mean, the senior students convey ideas to juniors, professors to their students, and even some websites facilitate the same. How can you say that what you are saying does not exist already?" I questioned.

"Remember, when you have an idea, it is quite possible that something related to it already exists or is being worked upon. Some answers to those problems/ideas/situations may also exist. When you try to solve problems or fill in the gaps of understanding, something already would also be filling that gap. It could be some preconceived notions, some basic research or work done on that, some unproven statements or myths, etc. It may not be a perfect gap, an empty hollow or a bare hole with nothing at all explaining it, but this does not mean something new, something better cannot take its place.

The earlier solutions or explanations may be of some help for the idea/problem/gap, but your solution could be unique, could be the one the world has been waiting for ever. Every person is unique, and has his/her own way of thinking and solving things in life. Some are good at certain things, some others at other things. Some explanations already existing should not be an obstacle for you to work out something great in the same area. In fact, if something already exists, there is also a possibility that there are several flaws with it, and it may be using numerous assumptions to solve the problem.

Before airplanes were invented, there were many theories as to why airplanes can't be built. And there were many other modes of transportation which worked just fine, and are used even today. Before the latest computers, as we see them today, were created, there were these old versions of them. These latest ones will get old when newer versions arrive. This process will keep going on. As the versions change, the customers also change or adapt. Initially, the first computers were as large as a room and very expensive. Slowly, as research kept going on, newer smaller and even portable versions came up. Now see, there are millions of computers built and sold around the world. Almost every house and office has a computer. Slowly, the laptops were invented. Now you can carry your computer everywhere you go. These things have happened and keep happening. Just see the growth of Microsoft Windows. Remember the old version Windows 98? And see, how through the years we now have an upscale, highly modern Windows 10. This does not mean there will not be any newer versions, they will keep coming up. If anything already exists, it does not mean that others can't work on that area. Windows is an OS, but it is not the only OS in the market. You have the very popular MAC OS, Linux etc. too. If someone had an idea earlier than you, does not mean you cannot have that or work on that too. You can still work on it in your own unique ways. As you did not have some good ideas while you sat around your home thinking, the same could be going on with many other students also, who suffer from the same problem. Remember, if there is any better solution to a question, it means it can replace or improve the previous solutions. It will definitely help mankind. A good solution or a better answer to an idea or a problem can come in as quick as days or may take as long as centuries.

"Centuries?" I asked.

He nodded, "Yes. See, it took centuries to answer the mysteries of the universe, to prove that earth is a sphere. Earlier people believed the earth to be flat, and that they could fall off the edge of the earth. But thanks to the great minds like Pythagoras, Kepler, Copernicus, Galileo, Newton etc., who filled those gaps with new, better, and logical solutions. Had they stopped working on the idea of finding more about the universe, its laws, etc. thinking that so much is already written in the old books, we may still be believing in those old myths.

Similarly, in today's world, there is this idea called air-conditioned mattresses. It is a concept of providing comfort to the human body while sleeping, using very less energy. Even in the 19th century, there were some solutions suggested by some scientists but those did not work, and even today researchers are trying to modify the concepts to find a solution. A company called Gentherm is doing very well on this. So you can't say that there are efforts already made regarding this and one should not try it, right?" he said. I nodded, and he continued, "Gentherm is doing well does not mean it has got all ideas behind it. It may have some good ideas, but it does not mean that would be everything. You can still come up with an idea to provide a better solution.

There are millions of patents granted. But no one can say that a better one cannot come up. It could even replace the previous one. If you go through any patents, even in your field, and find the claims made in them, you may be able to find some drawbacks in them, and you may even have a better idea than that. Nevertheless, remember, if you do not engage yourself in it, you will never come with that idea.

In 1899, Charles H. Duell, Commissioner of US Patent Office, said, "Everything that can be invented has been invented." But is that so? Not at all. The pattern of innovation is following the same course as it has been following since centuries. In fact, innovations may have increased and become even more valuable in our time.

The major question which sometimes comes in our minds is the probability of innovation coming from oneself. This is self-doubt. The doubt is not that innovations may not happen, it's about them not happening through us. Many times one runs through a self-check and finds that the probability of an innovation coming through him/her is very less maybe due to the lack of knowledge, proper resources etc., so to say, they are not yet ready to chase their ideas to innovations or inventions. Secondly, just like you, most people think, there are not enough opportunities to chase in their fields. But all these are your own obstacles, created by your own mind, leading you to think that you are not ready, or there are not enough opportunities. Normally students think that innovation is a result of talent, luck, hard work, and maybe, some other complex characteristics which they do not understand, or are simply out of their scope. Such thinking is not only negative but also wrong.

Usually, people think there are not enough opportunities to chase. For people like them, those who strive to 'only' pass the exams can never come up with great solutions or worthwhile answers to the real-life problems. But just think over, is that true? You can get thousands of examples of people who were college dropouts and did wonders. Actually, nowadays, it's quite easy to say there are a lot of opportunities to chase. Just by doing something new with any product or idea, many times, the process of using it or working on it changes. This change in the process may also be an idea or a solution towards the betterment of that product.

When you dive deeper into inventions, innovations, research papers, etc. you will find that they also use some other creations, at times more than one, on which their idea relies upon. They also use something which already exists. In the same way, as there are lots of inventions, innovations, and research papers coming out every day, they also have a chance of being used later in other such creations and wonders.

If I ask you to tell me some of the problems you have faced while working on your ideas, you may tell thousands. But basically, these can be categorized as two types – one, which can be solved, and the others, which cannot be solved. Those which can be solved may relate to you, to the things on which you can work upon, while the others, they may not be related to you – like scarcity of some resources, technical barriers, etc. If you search for ideas you will definitely find them, but it's up to you to choose to solve them or leave them as is.

Every field also has some emerging fields. For example, you are related to textiles. For you, nonwoven textiles may be an emerging field or textiles with nanotechnology could be another. There is no end of opportunities.

You are just starting your journey towards 'A', hence you feel uncomfortable and lack confidence. You may also be unaware of the practices you should follow to proceed with your idea. As of now, you don't have a prototype for your idea and haven't received any acclaim for that, could be a reason for your lack of confidence when you talk about your idea –that if someone asks, you have nothing to show. I have many ideas and I don't care if all of them are proven wrong. Even if all of them go wrong, I know how to get another one. It is not the idea alone which matters, it's a lot of execution which does."

Opportunity appears as dilemma

"Hi! On what topic you are going to lecture me today?" I asked as we met yet again one morning.

"You think I'm lecturing you?" he shrilled.

"No man, just kidding!" I laughed, "You have given me great insights into the world of innovation."

"Leave it. So tell me, have you been able to find an idea yet? Let me see if these 'lectures' are benefitting you or not," he said, emphasizing on the word 'lectures' sarcastically.

"I did get a few ideas, but I don't find them worth sharing. They don't seem good enough. And since I'm thinking a lot, I am too confused to zero in on one. All ideas seem fake. It is like a dilemma, the more I dive into the ideas, my dilemma of not being able to find something worthwhile increases," I said.

"Don't worry, it happens quite often until you make it real. It also means you are facing a challenge, and challenges are good to bring success.

The dilemma is something which hinders us to put in our best and reduces the zeal in our efforts to a great extent. With almost every opportunity we think of working on or even helping others, there comes a point of dilemma. All such points of dilemma need to be removed quite necessarily.

Another reason of arriving at points of dilemma is others' opinions about what we are doing or what we are about to do. Stages of dilemma

1. Dilemma while ideation.
2. Dilemma post ideation.
3. Dilemma during execution," he explained.

"Can you explain me these stages of dilemma?" I asked.

"Whenever you start thinking, you may encounter some dilemma. This dilemma happens because of the doubts or questions which remain unanswered in your mind. You always need to find the right question and then find an answer to it. Sometimes these doubts lead you to some philosophical questions which may be very hard for you to answer, and you may feel trapped. In such a case, you just need to do something with your idea that will answer most of the questions, even if not the current one. Slowly, things will unravel and all your doubts will clear.

When you are going through confusion while you start ideation, i.e. you have an idea but your mind is split between the decision of proceeding further or waiting for some doubts to be clarified, leading to some more dilemma points, one moment you may feel happy to have the idea, while the next moment you are in self-doubt. This especially happens when you discuss your idea with you friends, even your closest friends. The first time, when you have an idea, the dilemma starts popping up very soon. This may even be retained in your mind and hinder you later when you have moved on to new ideas. So it's very important to identify and stop the dilemmas from occurring.

You have to start working on your idea as soon as you get it. But to work on an idea needs some courage to proceed. When you have worked for some time and you review your work, you may start thinking if this idea will work or not = dilemma. Will your stupid actions lead to any invention, innovation or solution to real life problems? This is the dilemma of post ideation. In such a situation you need continuous mentoring. For this, you may either take help of a suitable person or, you may read the inspiring stories of others who worked an idea and came up with a solution. You may need to motivate yourself and be determined. You need to dig down deep into those inspiring stories. It will help you remove the dilemma of ideation.

Besides this, your thinking matters a lot while working on an idea. I will tell you how to go about the "something else" which you are looking for in your life. You don't need any technical knowledge for that, but it plays a very important role while working on 'A'.

When you test your idea, or maybe a prototype or concept verification of it by a particular method there is a chance that seeing the result you stumble and move away from working on it. This can be taken care of by the method of your execution.

In all these situations you stop working on your idea. You don't try to prove it right or wrong but you stop working on it because of the dilemma. Now, this is wrong. The situation of dilemma may also arise because of much brainstorming but no output which influences your emotions regarding your idea that – is it worthwhile, is it any good? So when you get an idea, don't get super excited, rather pause over it, think about it – it's practicality, use, and a way forward, else you may end up wasting a lot of time on a sunken ship and feeling embarrassed.

Remember, quitters start enjoying as soon as they get an idea, while winners start enjoying when they are actually working on it," he explained.

"I think what you are saying is right. Now I get the reason why I stopped working on my previous idea of converting the mechanical energy in shoes, while walking, into electrical energy. Dilemma made me stop!" I exclaimed.

"Many people come up with an idea which makes them feel they are going to be the next millionaires, they are going to bring a revolution for the mankind through their life changing formulae. They get a feeling of being superior to their colleagues and other people around them. But many of them regret later.

So many people, when they come up with an idea, enjoy it thoroughly without actually putting any efforts to think through it. They are even unable to write it down completely on a single page and think one day they will put it all down very clearly, without committing any mistakes. But things don't work like this. You ought to put some serious thinking to it, stay humble and work your way through before you start enjoying your idea," he finished, and that was the end of our meeting that day.

Myth:
There would be people
smarter than me

After a few days, Robin and I met again, one evening. "Hello boy, how's life going?" He asked.

"Nothing special, just passing the time. Since I have entered the college I have a feeling that life has gone to hell. I sometimes try to do things, but nothing works out. Thus I get more frustrated. Neither am I able to perform well at the things I want to do, nor in college.

I don't think someone like me can do anything in life. There are much better people than me who can perform well in each arena of life. There are people who are smarter than me. I can't concentrate on anything even for a single hour, so how can I do anything?" I replied, feeling dejected.

"Can you see that student?" he asked pointing towards a guy exercising in the park.

"Yes," I replied.

"I saw him a few days ago, while he was talking to a friend. As they were nearby, I could hear their conversation and I gathered that he is preparing for the undergraduate entrance examination. What do you think, will he be able to match you?" he asked.

"Why not? Do you think we study a lot? No. He can easily attain my level just by reading a few book. I think it would take him only a few months," I said.

"While discussing with his friend he mentioned he was a good student and a topper of the class. But for some reason, he is unable to concentrate on his entrance examinations. He also said that he has been thinking a lot about unable to study even a single hour whenever he tried to study. He said he got confused about what to study, what to leave and where to start. He discussed your college and said it is a good one where everyone gets placed in jobs. He wished of getting an admission in this college so that at least his life will be all set.

He can't even think of being compared to you. There are so many things he is struggling with. First, he needs to get an admission in the college, for which he needs to clear an entrance exam. Even after that, he needs to study a lot. If we think from his perspective, you would be far ahead of him.

Now let's change the things a little. Say we replace that student by you and you by someone who has already invented something or through his technical knowledge, has come up with something which is very useful for mankind. Now, that person looks at you and thinks you can easily do the same as he did, just by putting a little effort. And you, here, are thinking that it is very difficult for you and that you can't be compared to that person. So tell me, what is wrong here?" he asked.

"I don't know," I said.

He continued, "It's the feelings," he said, "They are sending the wrong signals. Remember, when Einstein gave his first theory on light, he was just twenty-one. There were so many people, probably much more knowledgeable, more educated, more aware and smarter than him, but it was he who came up with the theory. When Galileo gave his first answer about the earth revolving around the sun, then also there were people much smarter and knowledgeable than him. When the founders of Google came up with this search engine, do you think there were no other people on the earth as educated as or smarter than them?" I nodded, trying to imbibe each and every word. He continued, "It was the idea, their idea, and the right thinking which lead them to one of the online world's best creation ever - Google.

Even in your college, there would be a few students who would be much better than everyone else there. But among them, only a few may be able to be receptive to the signals of life, to the brilliant ideas they get and make a difference in the world. They are the ones to whom the society refers to as – 'Be like them!'

At this moment, if you go to your girlfriend and ask 'are there any people smarter than me? Even her answer could be such that you may start doubting yourself. My point is – it's not about being smarter or more educated, it's about being able to identify your ideas, put them through a practical and an appropriate thinking process, and work on them, rather than being only sentimentally attached to your ideas, without much thinking or action. Those who are able to do this, are the ones who make a difference in the world and are remembered.

We have proceeded very far in science but still lag behind in some important areas of life such as philosophy. We proceed with our life based on some assumptions. These are further based on our own life experiences, as well as those of others around us. A lot of these assumptions are also based on the already recorded theories and studies conducted till now, i.e. the books we follow. Some say that working hard is important, some say working smart is important. Some others say both are important. But no one as yet has come out with the best or fool-proof explanation. If you ask what is the definition of smart work you will find various explanations. So all this is relative. How far or how high you will go, is only up to you. You can seek assistance, support, and help, but in the end, it will always be up to you!"

Myth:
Complex technologies/solutions have more possibility to make people happy

"I think higher technologies or solutions have more possibility to make people happy. What do you think?" I asked.

"What do you mean by higher technology or higher solution? I am hearing it for the first time," he asked.

"I mean those technologies or solutions which have very complex algorithms, processing, theories, mechanisms, etc. running behind the scenes. I think only a few people are able to understand those, and highly technical people are required to work on them. For example, I am a textile undergraduate, if I came out with the solution which can make the yarn more uniform. Or I may come out with some dyes which can last much longer even though being a little expensive," I said.

"I guess by high technology or solution you mean the complexity?" he confirmed and I nodded, so he continued, "See dude, there is no relation between a complex technology or solution and happiness. They may or may not bring happiness to people. It's not about just that, it's about affecting the lives of people in a positive, progressive way. If you look at Facebook, starting Facebook wasn't so highly challenging or complex. If you read its story, it was just meant as a college fun thing. You may call it a low-level technology or solution, but see how it is affecting the lives of people all around the globe.

Most of the times you young students are driven by fancy projects and wish to work on them. But after some time, when you come to know that they may not play a big role in the society you lose interest. Remember, a complex product may not win the interests of common people. You may come up with a complex solution to bring the uniformity of the yarn but you have to remember it is not going to be an easy job for the operator thereon, you are not going to help him/her, or play a big role in his/her life. But coming up with some new type of fiber which may be more comfortable on people's skin could help you win hearts!

Remember, you can always avoid tasks for which many people are already putting in a lot effort. Given a chance, you should try to identify and work on things which very few people may get to work upon. Your experience may be good or bad, but it's always worthwhile.

Just a few years ago, even I was searching for an answer for this. As I started digging deeper I found that it is very different from how we generally think. Do you know what I realized? You don't need to be a Ph.D. or M.Tech. to come out with complex solutions to serve people. There is no connection between the happiness of the people and the complexity of a solution. It all depends upon the value of 'A' which you are going to work upon.

The complete solution which may serve mankind the best is generally a combination of low-level and high-level technologies, so to say complex and easy technologies, hand in hand."

Robin also gave a few examples of simple and complex solutions that can touch many lives:

Some examples of low-level solutions which may do wonders for others are:

1. Assume, a kid who came up with a process to save his/her cattle from wild animals, and the same being used for the whole village.
2. The design of Gabriele Diamanti about generating fresh water using solar energy.

Some examples of highly complex solutions touching millions of lives:

1. Mobile phones
2. Computers

Odon is a 59-year-old car mechanic in Argentina. He invented a mechanism for safely extracting babies stuck in the birth canal. His mechanism causes much less damage than any other method like forceps or suction cups. The idea came to Odon in a dream after viewing a video from YouTube. Were there not enough smart, well-educated doctors or biologists who could also do that? He wasn't even from that field. At a certain time when people may even be satisfied with the ideal methods of extracting babies through complex surgical procedures, he came up with an idea to make it easier and better.

So do you understand this or are you still confused?"

"Oh yes, I did understand quite a lot, but I think I will find some more stories so that I can be more satisfied and keep myself motivated," I returned bidding him goodbye. And so, when I came back I read umpteen number of stories to satisfy my mind.

Myth:
You can only DO well in those areas in which you are qualified

"Young boy, did you get any ideas to work upon?" he asked.

"No, not till now. I think there is nothing left in the textile industry to innovate. Whatever idea comes to my mind, I search it on the internet and I see that it already exists. Some ideas appear exactly the same as I thought, as if they just copied them while I was thinking!" I said.

"Can you tell me what you wanted to be before you joined this the college?" he asked.

"Why are you asking this?" I asked.

"You have not got a single idea till now, even after so much brainstorming and understanding, I don't think you had an interest in the textile industry. In fact, till now, I have not met anyone who actually had an interest in textiles," he joked.

"Hmmm," I sighed and said, "Actually I wanted to study aerospace. My dream was to be an astronaut. But I think, now I can neither be an astronaut nor can do anything in aerospace or any other field," I said.

"Young man, why are you so worried? I am sure there are much more things to do in textile. You are in one prestigious branch of humanity," he said.

"So? It does not have any relation with my interests. If there is something prestigious does not mean it must be my interest," I replied.

"Just kidding, boy," he smiled.

"This statement has got nothing to do with your choice of selecting the field in which you wish to explore. You can very well choose to work in the field of your interest by investing some more time to that. Although it is much easier to work in the area you chose to graduate, but, as we saw in the examples above, it's not mandatory. When you study, you learn much more than mere subjects, you gain knowledge about the working of various things in life. It will help you in some way or the other to follow your interests.

If you wish to explore the other field, analyze what you are going to lose while leaving the current career path.

Basically, you may lose some of the time you invested in learning or mastering the subject, not of your choice, which you could have very well put into the subject of interest. Let's say you lose a thousand hours. Think about it, any person can do that by working hard - ten hours daily for a hundred days. Not a big deal, is it? It's much less than putting your whole life behind something you don't want to do.

So if you don't switch to your interests now, all you will be saving is those hundred days, but what do you lose? Your interests, and your whole life doing something you never wanted to do. Not a big saving, right? In fact, you take lesser time to explore the field of your interest because you are passionate about it, have some basics of learning and generic knowledge already, and you are in a hurry. If you don't choose your interest now, you will lose even more time regretting your decision, doing nothing, as you anyways don't want to work on this subject. The actual loss of not choosing your interest would be much more than hundred days then. Making a mistake is not that big a problem than regretting not trying. One loses time, achieves nothing, and becomes weak, spending more time, making more mistakes.

There is a research which tells that only ten thousand hours are sufficient to make someone knowledgeable in any particular subject. Malcon Gladwell, in his non-fiction publication 'The Story of Success' mentions that 10000 hours of 'deliberate practice' are needed to gain world-class expertise in any field. I can say there are a lot of people who just invested one fourth of this, with their focused and smart work and achieved success. This is not the minimum time, it may even be less. So you can say - changing the career path is not a big deal if you are smart enough. I'll soon explain you about the smartness I am talking about – being smart at learning and being smart at work.

At present, technological advancements are playing a great role. Using these, the time required to acquire much knowledge has reduced many folds. As an example, the point which connects your technical knowledge to your practical knowledge is industry training which students only get in their third year. This is a barrier. One should get the practical knowledge right after technical knowledge. Students need practical knowledge in abundance, to be able to put their technical knowledge and theories into action. But due to the current system, one gets the much needed practical knowledge only after three years of studying theory. With almost everything at hand through the technological advancements, this time period can be reduced down to zero years.

Now, we can't say exactly how much knowledge is required to enter a new field, and you can very well enter it with zero knowledge, but without knowledge, you will have a lesser probability to innovate something in that field. It's not impossible, but it will need some well-focused hard effort, and during the course, you will also gain some good knowledge. When I say zero knowledge, I mean you have actually not studied it. For example, you have no knowledge of civil engineering, still, you may be able to bring out some innovation in that field because you are somehow connected with it in your daily life, although it will require some good hard efforts. Now say you want to innovate or bring about an application of nanotechnology. How can you do that if you have not even heard of this word?

In such a situation one may hardly be able to identify any application, theory or modification. He/she may only have a wish to explore it.

Let's say, you know a little bit about Nanotechnology, its uses, some applications or properties. Now, having some primary knowledge, one can at least start identifying a topic, an idea or a problem, which one wants to work upon. Maybe you want to build some good application around it. In fact, there are a lot of legends who started by working on some application of an idea or a subject and ended up providing great innovations.

Now, let's say, you have a good knowledge about the theory of Nanotechnology.

In such a situation one has full access to innovation. There are more chances of having some good practical ideas for innovation. Chances of excelling increase.

So if someone asks me, 'how much time it will be required for one to enter the arena of innovation in nanotechnology', I can say, maybe a few days of researching and studying on the internet or books. This time period is quite sufficient for one to at least start working on an idea to bring about an innovation in nanotechnology.

If you know the process of innovations you can very easily reduce your amount of 'B' (knowledge). But most of the people are not aware of it.

At the present, millions of people have lots of 'B' but they don't know how to use it. The question is, how those who have lesser knowledge in comparison to the experts come up with great innovation ideas, while the experts struggle with complexities?" he paused.

"Remember one more thing," he said.

"What?" I asked.

"I don't belong to the textile industry yet I can do something significant in this field. I don't belong to computer science, or chemical engineering, aircraft engineering, airspace technologies etc., but I can still do something significant in each of these fields. Even if you don't belong to food industry or medicine, yet you can do something significant there. By the way, you are an engineering student and it does not matter had you been a student of Bachelor of Science, the same thing would have applied to you even then," he said.

"Till now I thought I could work only in the fields which I was currently studying or will graduate in. Now I am able to see that link, how some people invented things in areas even when they did not belong there," I said.

Contributing to any part of the whole processing of 'A'

"What are you going to explain me today? Day by day, when I meet you, I am so excited to learn so much from you, things which no one has ever told before!" I said.

"What I am explaining you is just to push you when you need to think beyond the conventional thinking. Ok, tell me one thing, when was last time you helped a friend while studying?" he asked.

"I've helped my friends many times. This last time, a friend was trying to solve a complex numerical problem. He was just a step away from the solution, but somehow he could not see it. He was dejected and asked for help. I read the question, understood the numerical, and after some brainstorming was able to solve it for him. One can stumble in mid-way, even in such small problems," I said.

"Ok, give me an example where the opposite of this happened, that is, a friend of yours helped you solve a problem," he asked.

"This one time, when I was preparing for the undergraduate entrance exam, my friend and I would solve many questions together. Many times he was stuck in some questions and I would help him, while some other times, I was stuck and he helped me. But why are you asking this? Does it help in the process of

43

reaching 'A' in some way? Do you want me to work with any of my friends?" I asked.

He replied, "No, no, I am not asking you to have a partner in your idea. In fact, if you do so now, it may become a matter of dispute even before you come out with any significant solutions. Listen to me carefully. There are lots of people who are doing the same things or working on the same things, i.e., many people are trying to get 'A' and wish to have a solution for it. But most of them are not successful because they stop mid-way, maybe because of some problems or anything.

Just look at any industry and find a person who is skilled at numerous tasks of that industry. You will find that the CEO might be skilled in nearly all tasks of that industry. People at higher posts would either have numerous skills or would be exceptional at this one important task, for which they are well known amongst others.

Most of the people who wish to work towards innovation do not succeed because they have quite less understanding of people's requirements. This makes them less effective and prone to mistakes. Let's take an example - a person wishes to work on replacing the Air Conditioner with some other low-cost cooling solution. Now, if he/she discussed this with people, he/she may get the following information - Various facts about the environment, changing of temperature and humidity, cooling effect etc. Another person could tell him/her about the various limitations or restrictions in the way he/she is going to use/adopt it. Now here is a little advice for the upcoming innovators - they should only rely upon established and practically tested assumptions, facts and figures, and not the assumptions made by others no matter how talented they are.

Let's take another example - A person may have a lot of knowledge about solar energy. Say he/she comes out with solar panels having great efficiency, yet he/she may not be able to fulfill the requirement of the complete house, which was his/her aim. Now, he/she is dejected, but then, another person pitches in and tells him/her about the concept of redefined wattage consumption which can be used for a different purpose. Our innovator, working on a bigger solution, overlooked what he had created for a particular purpose may not be suitable for that but solved another problem. Just like cooling our body may not need a 60-watt fan, it could be done by maybe only a 25-watt fan. Similarly, the wattage of our televisions could be reduced by some innovation.

For any innovator working on a big picture, it might be somewhat difficult; if it could be partitioned, things become easier. That is why the most innovative organizations in the world, like IDEO, 3M, etc. hire a lot of innovators who collaborate or are put together in teams to come up with the best solutions.

Working in a team, everyone has a role. Some are good at problem-solving, some are technically very sound, some are good at suggesting alternatives, and some are good at intelligently testing the prototypes and listing what it lacks, some are good at explaining things to the teams working on the solution while some others are good at explaining things to the end users or customers, etc."

This book helps you in three areas

1. Knowing the myths.
2. Helping you find a topic to work upon.
3. How to proceed once you finalize the topic.

Myth:
Only I can do everything
in my 'A'

"You know, you don't need to do everything while working on an innovation. If you don't have any knowledge of computer science it does not mean you cannot think of apps," he said.

"Ok, but please explain me in detail," I asked.

So he explained, "There may be a huge amount of information required for a complete innovation. But it may also require 'something else' 'something more' to actually innovate. Most of the things (knowledge, skill, research, practice, etc. = 'B', as explained earlier) required for an innovation are already there with many people of that field, including your professors. If I take nanotechnology as a topic for innovation, there are so many experts, professors, students who already have 90% of things required for innovation.

Now, if someone else, someone like you with not enough 'B', is determined to go on the path of innovation, 90% of the information and knowledge can easily be provided to you through those who already know it. But the innovation you chose, may require the knowledge of two or more fields. It may require an understanding of combining different streams, and this is where it becomes quite hard because it's really difficult for one person to excel in all the areas. This also means you did not need 90% knowledge of only one stream. You need varying knowledge of various streams, and an ability or thought process to combine those and get a solution. Say, you may just need 20% knowledge of nanotechnology.

Take an example of a village man attempting to make an eco-friendly refrigerator run on conventional materials readily available and does not require electricity. His purpose may not be to freeze items, but just to store things of daily use in a place where he can keep them cool. Now, he does not have much knowledge about the thermodynamics, the cooling process, limitations of the material used for cooling purposes etc. He is just influenced by the fact that the contact of water with soil or coal or dried grass cool is good enough to serve his purpose of preserving the materials of daily life, keeping them cool. Now, anyone, even a fresh graduate like you could help him with some basics, he doesn't need to go in detail. Let's say he used coal, and comes up with a solution which works. He becomes an innovator! He can set up the same for others and help them.

But soon he finds that after prolonged use, his refrigerator is not cooling as much as it used to. Our innovator is in trouble. Again, a simple science student like you, someone with basic knowledge of working with coal, understanding the theory behind its cooling effects, could quickly analyze the situation and find out that it's just because of the blockage of the pores of coal after repeated use, its surface area reduced and the cooling is not up to the mark. You could explain the limitations of using coal, and he may think of using an alternative. So, even a fresh graduate like you seems to be an expert to him, who could explain him some basics to get on with this and solve his problems. Notice that he did not need the complex knowledge and theory about thermodynamics or other subjects to innovate something, or even solve his problems. He innovated, and you provided the required cushion through your basic knowledge.

Innovation, as we discussed earlier, is not about complexity, not about the complicated solutions or technologies, it's about solving problems or doing things in a better or easier way. It may only be for your own daily use, but could very well help others looking for a similar solution.

So any person with more 'B' as compared to the innovator can be very useful for the innovator. But there is a lack of a precise method for the flow of this information. At present, there are only a few sources like the incubation centers, IITs, National Innovation Foundation (NIF) Ahmedabad etc., but I feel there could be many other ways too, to make this information flow to the people needing help."

Ways of transferring information

This book illustrates various ways of transferring information. Most of the ways do not even need both the parties to meet. They may be connected with a common online source or by other means. A common place can help people from all over the world exchange information. Maybe a person from India has the same mindset to a person in China. They may exchange information through passages, statements, applications, etc., to aid each other.

Through passages - A passage is a written medium which has been explained in detail later. A passage on a topic contains information which can help in any part of the innovation. It may have certain explanations, descriptions, and even some research behind it. Any expert in a particular field can share his/ her knowledge by writing passages on the subject matter. There are so many people who can tell you about the areas which have a good potential for innovations. You may meet professors who can tell you about the topics of research or innovation in their fields, but they themselves do not pursue the same, maybe, due to lack of time, motivation, or their existing responsibilities. They may not be as eager to be part of innovations or research, but they can yield a good amount of written materials which can aid others who wish to tread the path of innovation.

Through statements - Statements are based on facts, analysis, results from experiments, and assumptions. These can either be proved or have been accepted as facts. They also show hidden possibilities of future innovation.

These are the two new ways readily available through the online world and provide much help in getting to 'A'.

Through something required – If you go by this method, to start with, you don't even need to find the 'A' yourself. You will get to 'A' through others' problems. Go to any entrepreneur or small business industry and you can easily find 'A'. Basically, it will be their 'A', but they may not be able to innovate things or processes because they focus is on their business and to get things done (innovating new ones may not be part of that). So focusing on their 'A' you have a possibility to come up with a solution, which may not only be helpful for them, but for others in that industry. So you arrive at 'A' using others ideas or problems, but you need to brainstorm a little more because these enterprises, especially the SMEs (Small and Medium Enterprises), hardly know what can make their business grow. You will have much more probability of getting success when you go to small enterprises, as bigger enterprises or organizations may have 'A' which may require much more manpower and resources to get to a solution. If you are just starting to find 'A' you are advised to go to SMEs.

Opportunities in unfinished innovations - These are those opportunities, wherein the 'A' is already there, someone thought of it, but never finished working on it, for any reason. Every innovator or inventor has an 'A'. So there are ample amount of PSIO (Problem Specified Incomplete Opportunity). These are similar to - when your friend comes to you with his problems, but here, you will receive these problems from completely unknown people.

Documentation

"**D**o you write your ideas on paper or diary?" he asked.
"Usually I don't write. I used to have a diary and wrote a couple of ideas in it, but nothing more. I think when I can remember them, why do I need to write? They are neither in syllabus nor need to be recorded," I said.

He shook his head and said, "You may be missing an important step here. And this may be one reason why you are not able to get a breakthrough. Documentation is a very important step for 'A'. Innovation is a time-consuming process. Although it depends upon the project, it does take some time to complete the whole process.

I say it's a time-consuming process because:

1. The 'B' required to fulfill 'A' takes time.
2. Brainstorming on the solution takes time.
3. Brainstorming requires something 'else'.
4. Experimentation takes time.

Usually it takes months or even years to complete the process and finally, come up with the optimized innovation. While brainstorming, you may have many ideas, but at that time you are not sure which would be the best one. So, their collection becomes quite necessary. Amongst them, some will be worth keeping, some can be struck off. The ideas which strike your mind for the first time may even take years to come again. So it's wise to note them down. Everything which comes to your mind, even for a short time, may have some potential to find a breakthrough or at least solve some problems, and must not be lost. It's just like dreams we see during our sleep. At times, we do remember them as soon as we wake up, but through the day, we tend to forget what we saw. But if you keep thinking about them through the day, or note them down, you will remember them. The cause of forgetting the dreams is losing focus from them over the day, the lack of reminder at various intervals, or the lack of their record. So if you keep remembering them through your day, focus on them all the time or note them down, you won't forget them for a very long time. Now, someone may ask - what is the relation of dreams to documentation? When you are living to innovate, you must not leave anything unturned. If there anything worthwhile in the dream, that must also be documented. There have been many instances where a solution came to the inventor in a dream. So you should be smart enough to gather whatever you can, anything that can help you achieve your innovation, then be it an idea, some knowledge, a conversation with someone or even a dream.

Besides this, one point worth noting is the dying of ideas. When an idea comes to your mind, but it is lost, it hinders your thinking a lot. You strive and struggle to regain it, and once you fail, you stop trying to think more. The idea is as good as dead because it doesn't exist anymore. Neither did you note it down nor do you remember it now. It's a great hindrance in the path of innovation.

I'll give you an example. You have solved a hard problem in physics or math, and the final solution you came up with, was very similar to something you had thought of earlier. But because you never noted it down, you couldn't go back to it and had to devise it all again. It's like re-inventing the wheel all over again. So noting down your ideas, solutions, etc. is of utmost importance and comes out very handy to solve your problems, as and when you encounter them.

This happens because we are never taught in schools to document things like ideas, thoughts, etc. We are just taught to document knowledge to get high grades. Imagine, if you do not document or take notes in your school days, what would happen... you tend to get low grades or have difficulty in understanding and learning things. You do all that for your education. Similarly, on your path to innovation, you must follow the same process. Note down ideas, possible solutions, logics around them, etc. all you can think of. The more you have in writing, the clearer your mind will be able to see further. You can keep going back to your notes to recapitulate your thoughts, to keep reminding yourself of your ideas. Not documenting will make you do things again and again, and at times you may have to start all over again, from the beginning.

Most people have many ideas at an early age. I guess children, howsoever impractical, have the most ideas. But all these are lost due to lack of documentation.

There could be many viable methods to document all that comes to the mind. It could be writing in a diary, taking pictures or drawing diagrams, etc.

For easy documentation I will tell you about the ABCD formula which will give you the required space for writing each and every thing that comes into your mind. It is not a new formula scientist have been using for a long time.

I think you remember what 'A' and 'B' are. Soon I will explain you 'C' and 'D' and together you can use these as the 'ABCD' formula or rule which is very effective to move towards innovation. Even scientists have been using this for quite some time. Documentation is necessary at each step – 'A', 'B', 'C' and 'D'. So, for easy documentation, thanks to the technological advancements, I will give you a method, a tip, which will enable you to record your thoughts very easily, without putting much time or effort, and will definitely increase your productivity. You can very well use pen and paper but I'd suggest you use an application for documentation. Nowadays, everyone uses a mobile phone, and there are tons of productive applications for this purpose.

In the app one will be able to:

1. Instantly secure what comes to your mind.
2. No brainstorming required on where to write it or how to secure it.
3. If the thoughts lead to a huge documentation record which can be useful as a knowledge resource, one can very well publish his/her work in the form of a book.
4. You can easily track your project and thoughts on a daily basis, even after decades. It's categorized and managed for you, so you won't lose it, and you don't need to go and search your cupboards for this.
5. You can easily share the information with someone you want to, even your children.
6. You can easily store the reference links, say even from Wikipedia or other knowledge sites.
7. it's so easy to create a database of all the ideas which come to the mind, even if they are a thousand in number. They will be there and never lost.

If you read about successful people like Albert Einstein, Leonardo da Vinci, Nikola Tesla, Robin Sharma, etc. – they always documented their ideas.

In my opinion, always carrying a notebook can be cumbersome. You always have to write in a specific manner, you need to update it regularly. It's difficult to organize and arrange ideas. All you can do is append more text to the already written one. But in this digital age, you are free to try out and use apps to organize your thoughts and ideas. The important thing is – to actually note down your ideas, no matter how you do it. Apps make it easier, but it's up to you if you are a pen and paper person.

Earlier, people used to talk to each other, they would take an appointment or identify a time when the other person would be free to talk. With technological advancements, now we have WhatsApp. You can easily contact others, and they can respond whenever they are free. Oh yes, SMS was also an option, but do you see the innovation here? SMS existed already, there was no problem with that, but how WhatsApp came in and replaced it. I'm sure you prefer WhatsApp over conventional SMS, for the ease, security, features, and options provided by it. We don't have to pre-plan the discussion. Similarly, ideas have nothing to do with your schedule and can come at any time. Hardly any people keep their ideas in written form. Only the wise do so."

Strength of unproved statements

"Do you have any assumptions of your own regarding science?" he asked.

"What kind of assumptions?" I asked.

"When you try to innovate something you start with some assumptions, which we can also refer to as statements. These statements play an important role in getting 'A' and its solution. For example, say, I am working on the air conditioned mattress so I may have many assumptions or statements like 'we spend lots of energy to cool down the human body' 'we can provide cooling effect while one is sleeping on a surface' 'we need more cooling effect while sleeping' etc. So, do you have any such assumptions or statements written anywhere?" he asked.

"Yes I had a few, but I never wrote them anywhere," I replied.

"Do you remember some of them? Can you tell me a few?" he asked.

"When a person moves, while walking, there is a certain amount of energy available, which I think can be stored. I only remember this," I said.

"Not having a good basis, so to say assumptions or statements, to start with 'A' is a big fault. Do you know how many platelets are required for a human to survive?" he asked.

"Nearly 1.5 lacs," I replied.

"Do you think anyone can survive with a few thousand platelets?" he asked.

"No, I don't think so," I replied.

"You wish to get answers for your 'A' but don't even have ten statements regarding it and you think you can do something remarkable?

You know, most of the inventions and innovations took place only because of the unproved statements which came into their minds at first. Unproved statements are just assumptions which one has in mind. These come into the mind because of his/her experience with science, surroundings, observations, etc., and these experiences differ from person to person. For example, some of the students may conclude their experience with - working on science is too tough and hard, while some may have had a great experience and conclude - working on science is very interesting.

Similarly, someone may say that nonwoven textile can also be explored in wallpaper field, someone may believe that there can be some extraordinary application of a particular proven theory.

There can be two types of unproved statements – personal and scientific.

Some examples of personal unproved statements are:

1. One should work very hard. This is a belief, an assumption, but it is not necessary that hard work will definitely lead to success. There have been people who've done quite a lot of hard work, yet failed.
2. One must always achieve a high grade in the examination. We assume that achieving a higher grade in exams leads us to success, but it cannot be proved and there are cases which tend to differ.
3. Tell a lie whenever it is necessary, maybe for something good. This is a very personal opinion, choice, and belief. It may or may not hold good.

The scientifically unproved statement could be, if you can change something into a liquid and preserve it, you can sell it. The below diagram shows that some proved and unproved statements can lead to the required answers/solutions/ innovations. If these do not suffice, we work on the requirement, find more things, maybe prove some unproved statements, add, more and more proven and unproven statements and keep adding them through our work, research, etc. till we solve the problem or find a solution for 'A'.

Driving force generation

"What is this driving force generation?" I asked.

He explained, "Whatever you choose to do you need some motivation for it. Usually, we start doing something if we have some motivation to do that. We are good, we feel motivated and generally, are able to accomplish it. In certain cases, if what we want to do is going to take a long time, we need a regular dose of motivation, otherwise, we may lose interest mid-way and stop doing or progressing with the task. This motivation is the driving force. You need some kind of force to do things, and motivation is just that force, hence it is called the driving force. For just passing an examination, you may need only a little driving force or motivation, and it could be that you are able to proceed to the next class, or you do not get scolded by your parents. But in case you wish to come first among some thousand students then, this little bit of motivation won't work. You will need a regular dose of a substantial force to drive you continuously and bring the zeal to work hard with perseverance and determination to achieve success.

Whatever we do in our daily lives is the result of some driving force. We have some motive behind all our actions. Many times we may say a driving force is not required for some necessary things like living your life; many people live their lives without having a specific motive in their minds. But it may not be true for everyone. Now, I hope this never happens to anyone, but when someone loses a close one, it becomes really difficult for the family members to endure the pain. This is when they start supporting each other to cope up with the loss and drive each other to carry on with their lives. They become a motivation for each other. If they do not do this, soon they are going to be in depression and may not be able to live happy healthy lives.

Having an idea and working on it is like having a family member who relies solely on you for a life. If you do not have enough driving force to work on it, it's going to die. To keep up the motivation, the driving force behind your work you may have to fight, fight with your own thoughts and emotions. Many times you will be attacked with thoughts which say that your idea is not right, it does not have enough strength to help the world, and you would think the idea is good but you do not have enough strength to complete it. All this is going to end up in a dying idea, a dying 'A'.

Generally, there is a pattern of thoughts which form in the mind while innovating. The good thing is - it can be predicted!

At present, most of the students emphasize greatly on 'B' but ignore 'A' and 'D'. Oh well, I haven't discussed 'D' yet, but let's say it's anything apart from knowledge ('B') that aids 'A'; it can be an idea, a product, a statement, an assumption, a theory or principle, just anything that will help you on your way to innovation on the decided topic ('A'). It's kind of a refined form of 'A' that takes you closer to the answer. I'll discuss more on this later.

When you have any idea, doubts are bound to come up. These may arise because of your own thoughts, doubts, and lack of confidence, or because of others' opinions. Many times these doubts or questions have a devastating impact on the idea and make us skeptical of something we once believed in with such fervor.

There are some basic questions which come to the mind initially. Some of these come to every innovator, while some others depend on the idea.

The questions themselves are not the worst part, it's the innovator trying to avoid these instead of answering them. Actually, these question may not be that easy to answer. Many could be philosophical or based on beliefs or assumptions yet to be scientifically proven. It is quite hard for one to answer why no one else thought of that same thing; and if someone thought of it, then why he/she could not explore and invent or innovate something over it."

As per my discussions with him, which I kept as notes and put them in the form of this book, some of these questions will be answered for you, here, in a raw manner. Some of these questions will be answered in a later edition. But you need to understand, if you want to be the leader, the innovator there is no running away from the questions and the obstacles that come your way. You need to dig, fight, and find the answers and pave your way forward.

These basic questions are most difficult to answer. Maybe someday, someone will be able to find answers to these in a very easy way, which everyone could believe in.

Some people fail to implement or execute their ideas even after having lots of 'B'. This happens because they fail to answer the basic questions which arise in their minds. Also, they fail to acknowledge that all knowledge does not come from schools or colleges. This additional knowledge is very important for being the innovator to achieve excellence and reach the pinnacle of your abilities. How do you attain this? You earn it through experience, practice, and staying steadfast on your path.

In addition to the basic doubts and questions, there are some more which solely depend on the idea. They come into the mind while processing an idea or working on it.

Through the unique methods explained in this book, you will be able to identify the right questions and will be able to answer them. The method we will use is to focus on the task and answer the questions at hand. This will relieve you of many questions even before they pop up in your mind.

The continuous answering of questions helps you concentrate fully on the topic ('A') and the idea, reducing the possibility of leaving them aside and making this whole process an enjoyable one. This also saves a lot of time. In such a situation, if one does leave an idea, he/she would definitely have a valid reason behind it. It is notable that at present, many people who leave their idea have no valid reason behind it, which is unfortunate.

You know when this is about to happen to a person who was very excited when he/she had the idea to work upon, but now, when you ask how it is going, he/she replies, "Haanji, theek hai, kaam chal raha hai (Yes, it's fine, work is going on)."

Continuous success is very important to keep the driving force in action and it doesn't matter how big or small the success is, or if it is real or virtual/pseudo (Virtual or pseudo success means it may not directly help you achieve your final goal, but it brings positive vibes to you and motivates you to work harder and remain steadfast on your path. These are basically the positive signs you see on your way to the final goal).

Examples and ways of having continuous success:

1. It is a good idea to break down your goal into smaller chunks and keep measuring your success from time to time through the successful completion of these, as you progress through the various stages of reaching your final goal.
2. Virtual success – Increasing subscribers of Robin Sharma made him believe in himself. It kept him motivated to strive for excellence and move forward with his goals.
3. Virtual success – Assume a boy loves a girl but is not sure if she has the same feelings for him. His friends suggest there is no point running behind her. Initially, he stays steadfast on his path and does his best to show his affection and care for her. Soon he sees some positive response from her. Now, he hasn't reached his ultimate goal of acquiring her love, but he sees a little success, some positive signs (each sign being a virtual success for him), which helps him put even more efforts and progress towards inculcating the feeling of

love for him, in her. But in case, soon he sees that the girl is definitely trying to ward him off, or avoid him, and has no interest in him, he can set aside the idea of putting in more time and effort for the cause.

Similar is the case with a difficult project. No one has even tried it, but they say that it's a waste of time and it may never work out. But you are steadfast. You want to make it work, so you start putting in efforts which start bringing in a positive response. That's your virtual success, people start believing in you.

4. Research for yourself and see how the latest innovative companies work. All rely on the milestones, the checkpoints which they have marked to see if they are on the path to success or are they straying away from it.

Every success adds to our courage which can help us sustain any possible failures ahead.

Pseudo/virtual success: As seen from the examples above, this may not exactly be a real success, but a positive pointer, where the author feels the positive signs and takes them as a little success towards his final goal.

Pseudo/virtual failure: It is the exact opposite of the pseudo-success. Here the person gets negative vibes and starts feeling he/she may never reach the ultimate goal, or it may never work out. It's the feeling of failure, and may not be a direct failure of the end goal, but an in between step which did not work out. It could even be negative responses over the work demonstrated by the person. Pseudo failure can be dangerous and without actual proof, could lead the person to set aside his/her goal. So, it's important that he/she does a quick analysis to see what went wrong, rather than feeling demotivated from the temporary failure. Well, for the negative response from others, it could be that the person was not able to put across his points/theory to others in the right way, maybe he/she needs to explain this to others in another way, so that they are able to see the same thing, or even work out something new which will make it clearer.

Pseudo-success can be helpful but during pseudo failure, it's important to believe in yourself. Many people are left devasted and quit after these pseudo-failures. One should remember, these do not mean ultimate failure. This was just a step that did not work. Think of other steps, other ways to do it. Don't quit unless you have a logically proven reason that your idea will not work.

The methods illustrated in this book make the whole process of innovation quite interesting, protecting the enthusiasm of the person and keeping him/her motivated throughout. It also helps to make the process of documentation pretty easy and straightforward. Anyone can easily save that and proceed further whenever required, be it an ABCD file with papers or an app having forms in the form of ABCD. The process of innovation can sometimes become very lengthy where a person may encounter a gap of a couple of years or more. In such a case, when one wants to start again, he/she must have all old documents available. People who constantly indulge in the activities of innovation do this but students mostly ignore this crucial step leading to failure and dying of their ideas.

Statements are data sets, a set of points, best to set the boundaries for the process. The innovation will be around these set of points. It is necessary to know what are the limitations, current advancements, and future possibilities etc. as these clearly state those boundaries up to which one is ready to and can go. 'No one can convert the solar energy falling on a unit area more than a certain amount.' Now, this is a statement, correct to a certain degree as of now, defines a limit, but a future innovation may change everything. So statements are the boundaries and basis for now, but they do have a possibility to change. Let's go through another statement 'If you can create and package food which tastes better than the one's currently available and improve its shelf-life, i.e. it can be preserved for a longer duration of time, you have a lot of opportunities to come out with great solutions of selling foods'. There are lots of statements which have been given in detail in the statement section. The above statement tells a good amount about the selling of food or innovation in the food industry.

Passages can have a lot of ideas woven together. Unlike statements, which sound pretty much straightforward and objective, statements are descriptive and give a detailed account of one or more ideas or topics. This book in itself is a passage, an essay, a step-wise guide on how to go about innovation. It explains you everything about innovation from finding your 'A' to the end of innovation. Now, it may not be possible for anyone to read out all the passages related to a single topic as innovation may require some directly related passages as well as indirect ones. So, whenever anyone gets something which can maintain his/her desire to innovate, it could be much different than a 300-page book. You can easily get access to the online information these days. One person interested in innovation can easily go through 4-5 passages a day. You may easily go through the passage section and find out the ones helpful to you.

The driving force, like gravity, is that invisible power which has the capability to pull all your focus and bring the best out of you. The quicker you find the answers to your questions the greater this force will be. The more answers you get, the less you will stumble and remain high on motivation. Some may object and say 'I have seen/read about many scientists who waited for a very long time for their quest and never lacked the motivation.' I'd say that one may wait for a long time for a single answer but not for a bunch of questions, especially in the initial phase. Those bigger questions come into the picture once the stage is set, once you are on your way to working out a solution."

"You know one thing?" Robin asked.

"What?" I replied.

"Whatever I have told you about 'myths', 'retarders', etc. these are just a few examples. All of these may not be the most well-known or the biggest problems, but what I want you to understand is that on this path you will come face to face with many of these, and it's really important that you overcome them. You are not the only one who has to face them, each and every innovator, inventor, research, and entrepreneur faces it, then be it a noble prize winner or a billionaire entrepreneur.

Thomas Edison, the inventor of the electric bulb had a myth - DC current is the future of the world. When Nikola Tesla went to him with an alternative project on the electric current, he rejected it saying the project had no future. Later he found it was the biggest mistake. When Galileo proposed the concept that earth moves on its own axis, he got a punishment because there was a myth that whatever is written in ancient books cannot be wrong no matter what proof you gave. If you talk about specific retarders and myths I would like to tell you about an incident which took place after the invention of red and green LED bulbs. There was a strong requirement of the Blue LED bulbs. It was a myth that the Blue LED cannot be made because it needs the use of a semiconductor with an Eg of approximately 2.6 eV or more, while most commonly used semiconductor, silicon, has the value as 1.1eV. It took decades to make a Blue LED.

There are a few myths, which may be statements or assumptions in the current time and may take centuries to be actually known as 'myths', some take decades to be proven otherwise and mark those earlier statements as 'myths', some take reading of a few books to know they are just 'myths', some take as little as a conversation with someone (a friend, a professor etc.) to understand they were just 'myths', while some may take just a few seconds to know it they were a myth (while solving problems of say maths, physics, chemistry, etc.). But you know what's interesting?"

"What?" I asked curiously.

"Many of us take years to know that some of the statements we believed in are myths. These could have been realized, maybe, just by reading a few books. This also happens because of 'rumored reality', statements which we have heard from here and there, but only start doubting them after a very long time, when we have gained some experience or knowledge of our own," Robin stopped. His bag was packed, it was time. He was leaving for about two months to go out of India for a project, but I wanted to know more. He looked at the clock and asked, "Do you want to say something?"

"Oh, yes. I would like to wish you the very best for the completion of your project. It is a great pleasure for me to be with you. I just love listening to you. What is the last advice you would like to give me before you go? What should I do regarding these 'myths', 'retarders' etc.," I asked.

He didn't say anything. He nodded and we started coming down the stairs to the road where his cab was ready to go. He opened the door, paused, and said, "Concentrate hard to find the answers to your questions which are hindering you from finding your idea, or working on 'A'." With that, we waved each other goodbyes, see you later, and he left.

Section-2

Passage

"How are things going Raj?" Ankit asked sitting on the famous ladder. There is a place in our hostel where we used to sit during our free time. We did get a lot of free time, yet it seemed too less when we were in college. Ankit was one of the most disciplined students of our batch.

"Nothing special, everything's going as before. What about you?" This was a standard reply to this question. Meanwhile, I looked at my watch. There was still enough time to go to meet Robin. I was excited.

Ankit: Everything fine, just a little unwell these days. So, what happened to your project?

Me: Which project?

Ankit: Hey, the one in which you won a prize.

Me: Oh that one. I have just paused it for a while.

Ankit: Buddy, you are the only one doing something good. Finish it man, so that we also get to proudly say that we know someone who has done something great. Is there any problem you are facing in that?

Me: Actually I need to perform an experiment for that, but that's very expensive, so am trying to find an alternative solution.

Ankit: I too have an idea, but...

Me: But what?

Ankit: You know buddy, how much knowledge we need to work on anything. Also, whenever I look it up over the internet, so many people have already done many similar things. Although my idea is a little different but looks like all innovations have already been done.

I just felt he was going through the same phase as I had been through once. That was the time when Robin came as a savior. Guess it was my turn now. So I explained to him what all I had learned from Robin.

Ankit: Hey why are you looking at your watch again and again? Is someone waiting for you?

Me: Oh no, I have some important work.

Ankit: Oh yeah, why not, work is always important.

He said it tauntingly as if I was going to meet my girlfriend.

Me: Hey, nothing like that man.

Ankit: Alright alright. No need to give explanations. Go wherever you need to go. Thanks for the talk, by the way. I'll think over what you have told me.

And so, I left to meet Robin, after a long time.

"Hello dear, how are you?" He welcomed me with a warm smile.

Me: I'm fine, thank you. What about you, how was your trip?

Robin: I'm good too. Yes, my trip was good, had a great time and the project was a success.

Me: So, what you are going to tell me today?

Robin: I have already explained you about the myths and retarders. Hope you are working on them and exploring as much as possible. Now I am going to tell you about how to get 'A'. These are the methods which I have learnt through various experiences in due course of time. Remember I mentioned about 'passage' earlier? I am going to explain that in detail.

The passage is a written material which we can go through in a single read. It's like an essay. It may vary in length, but it's not like a book that you need days to go through it. A passage is complete in itself, but you may have a number of passages to connect the dots and get a bigger picture. A passage would typically have a beginning or an introduction, a description of things or views and opinions and an ending or a conclusion. This mode of getting knowledge from or noting down in the form of passages is not new, and knowingly or unknowingly you would have already been using it for various purposes. The articles you read in a newspaper or a magazine are all passages. Even the articles available on the apps of your phone, like the ones on YourStory, or on the internet, are all passages. These passages contain information. This information may be problems, suggestions, solutions, assumptions, views or opinions, advice, an account of some incident which took place, stories, explanations, etc. All these are required for getting 'A' and its answer.

"Why a single read is important?" I asked.

"A single read is important because you never read the NOT SO IMPORTANT things multiple of times. Do you read the same news in the newspaper for the second time or multiple times? Definitely not. Also, if the newspaper has a single article on the full page, would you read?" he asked. "Definitely not, who will waste so much time. But for the purpose of getting to 'A' and its solution, I think I can do that too," I chuckled.

He joined in with his laughter and said, "Now, if you've read the newspaper, will you be able to tell about the total number of deaths mentioned in it? Perhaps not. But if you start reading it just keeping in mind about total deaths, you may be able to come up with an answer with some accuracy."

"Have you read any journals?" he asked. "No, I tried many times but I find them very uninteresting," I said.

"So, if I go and read a passage about my problem, I may come up with its solution very soon?" I asked.

He shook his head and replied, "No, it's not that easy. You cannot get 'A' and its answer that easily. You need to concentrate on lots of 'A's or topics. For this, you need various resources from different sources and time for collection. You need to be prepared well. Many have the capability to collect passages which may be helpful to them at some stage but once you've zeroed in on your 'A', you start drawing your 'ABCD' chart.

A = Topic.

B = Knowledge around that topic.

C = Conclusion or inferences from the knowledge (We'll come to this later).

D = A refined idea, product, requirement, problem statement you are going to solve, etc. → Similar to 'A'.

When you draw your ABCD chart you can identify the passages you need to proceed further and the ones you don't. You keep the needed in your collection. Now, whatever you collect here is your shortest path towards your 'A' and its answer or solution."

"Then why are passages so less seen on the path of innovators? I haven't heard much about these," I said.

He smiled and said, "Average students like you have a great potential to get to 'A' and its solution but you have been ignoring the power of passages. Innovators, inventors, and researchers have already been using them. I'll tell you a story.

Robert Fischell has attained more than 200 patents. One night he was reading a magazine when he stumbled upon an ad for a pacemaker battery, bragging about how it lasted for two years. You know how he responded to that? He said, 'wait a minute - this thing is in somebody's chest! It lasts for only two years and they are proud of it?!' At that time, people with pacemakers had a surgery every other year to get their batteries replaced. He thought, 'what we need is a tiny nickel-cadmium cell on a coil of wire inside the pacemaker that is rechargeable by magnetic induction through the skin. It would last the patient's lifetime'.

Fischell allocated a group of engineers in his Applied Physics Lab at John Hopkins University to create a prototype. It was not only rechargeable but also smaller than the existing model."

"Wow! What an incredible person, 200 patents. If I had so many patents I would have lot more in my life, including a girlfriend," I laughed.

"Not one dear, you could have many," he laughed.

"Can you tell me, why you young students feel so lucky to have a girlfriend? What do you get from her?" he asked teasing me. "A lot actually. It's a great feeling, I don't know how to explain it in words. I think it gives excitement, contentment, pleasure. And then there comes a point when we start searching for OYO Rooms," I blushed.

"What do you do when you are sitting with your fast friend talking about something interesting? I mean, do you remember your girlfriend or you just enjoy talking to your friend?" he asked. "Just enjoy talking to the friend. In fact, I enjoy that a lot. I don't know if the point is worth the time or not, I mean life is not about talking everything only if it has some worthiness. If I am enjoying the talk, then it's good. And I can't live only to remember her all the time," I said.

"Passages are the same, they are like your friend-1, friend-2, friend-3, etc. and every passage represents something in itself. I'm talking about all the passages you would have collected for your 'A'. It's like all of you are talking to each other and discussing on a single topic. And I think you would enjoy such a discussion. If you love processing information it means you have great potential to be an innovator, an inventor or someone who has an 'A' and its solution," he said.

Here, I'll give you a passage for better understanding:

Using artificial intelligence (AI) for image classification and object recognition is not new. Many techniques and sophisticated software have been developed over the past decade to do just that. Extending some of the well-established machine learning techniques to three dimensional images such as those made by micro-CT is a new challenge.

Image classification may be performed using supervised, unsupervised, or semi-supervised learning techniques. In supervised learning, the system is presented with numerous examples of images that must be manually processed and labelled. Using the training data, a learned model is then generated and used to predict the features of unknown images.

Over the past fifteen years, the X-ray CT machines at the department of Applied Mathematics have been busy producing thousands of 3D images. A 3D image may be composed of multiple elements, minerals, alloy etc. Separating these components can be challenging and is certainly a laborious manual task in 3D.

In this project, the students will be working closely with the researchers to implement machine-learning techniques for material identification in 3D images."

He then asked, "Can you tell me what you understood from this passage?"

"This is a somewhat boring topic for me and I understood only one thing that the machine learning techniques to get three-dimensional images such as those made by micro-CT are a new challenge and nothing else," I said.

"Congratulate yourself. You have 'A' although it would be very tough for you to get its answer. Do you have an interest in mathematics?" he asked.

"Huh! It cannot be so easy! If it so then I can tell you lots of such 'A'. I don't think it is so impressive to get such an 'A'. I mean solving them is also a big thing," I said, "And yes, I have an interest in mathematics. Do you want to say that as this project uses mathematics, and I have an interest in mathematics, so I also have the ability to solve it?" I asked.

"Yes, definitely! That's the point," he said.

"I think students of applied mathematics would be better at it as they have spent 3-4 expert years on it. They have more probability to solve this than anyone," I said.

"There were many scientists who published papers for the theory of photoelectric effect. There were many scientists who had been working on the conversion of cellulose into petroleum before Sujay Tyle presented his work when he was just nineteen years old. There were many scientists who had worked upon and published their works before the inventor who invented the Blue LED!" he exclaimed.

"Whatever field you choose, there will be enough people who have lots of knowledge and a better probability of getting to 'A' and its answer than you. But that should never stop you from following your path. Ok, you may not work on above 'A' because you don't have enough interest in the field or are not sure how you will get access to the facilities required for this, but not because there are other people who know more than you," he said.

"I think now I'm getting some clues as to why I can work in this field," I said.

"Ok, let's have one more passage then:

Since my childhood, I have seen many changes in the structure of my house. Many times various faults happened due to which the construction had to be done again by breaking the existing structure. By doing so, a lot of money was wasted. If there had been a little knowledge about the designs and stuff, things may not have gone so bad. In addition, it would have been the best possible design that we could get.

The budget of a middle-class family which wishes to construct a house is not that great, resulting in a house which generally lacks the good appearance it could have had. Some middle-class families don't even know that there are expert designers who design the whole house in the best possible way. The problem is not that they don't know about this, but it's the cost associated with hiring a designer. Besides, searching for a good designer is a daunting task, especially if the member responsible for getting things done is not aware of the internet.

There are lots of manufacturing companies who manufacture good quality things from some of the cheapest materials available for construction and interior decoration purposes. But they have to go through various middlemen before reaching their end consumers, which makes the cost of even these cheap products so high.

"So, would you like to say something about the above passage?" he asked.

"This seems quite easy to understand. And I think it is true about most problems faced by an average Indian family. In this passage, it is being said that people face a lot of problem regarding the interior design of their house. Many are not even aware of the experts who can help, then even if one hires an expert, the costs may not be bearable for a simple middle-class family. All in all, they end up wasting a lot of their hard earned limited money, yet they are unable to get the best they actually could get. I think if there could be some apps which could help people in designing their homes, won't it be better?" I said.

"You young guys only think about apps. Think more, come up with something better. Apps cannot do everything. You may enjoy that you have got an idea for your 'A', but the problem is that you people make conclusions very fast that it will solve the problem or is the perfect solution. You have just taken your first step, you are yet to encounter a hundred more," he said.

"But do you think the 'A' which we find from the above passage needs a complex solution? It can definitely be a simple app?" I asked.

"You may come up with a complex solution or you may just find an easy one. It all depends upon your thinking. Most people may come up with apps, but some may find new ways of construction or designing which are easier and cost less. Some may even give free advice for making a house. Twenty years ago people in India had almost no access to the internet, but now you have good access and a lot of audiences, which has even changed the way of earning. Even by giving information for free, you can earn by other methods like ads," he added.

"So you say that each and every article in the newspaper and magazine is bound to have 'A'? Does it mean I should read each and every article to find my 'A'? Don't you think it will be too much?" I asked.

He shook his head, "You don't need to do that. But you just need to change the way you read the articles. Firstly, till now you used to read articles without any expectation. From today you need to read them attentively and focus on them until you get several ideas. Once you get these ideas, you need to collect more passages around them, so to say, 'related articles'. All will be ultimately related to your 'A', whenever you find it.

Secondly, you need to concentrate more on the passages oriented around the problems and the challenges around those ideas. From here, you should be easily able to zero in on your 'A', the topic you want to work upon, the problems you want to solve or the answers you want to find."

Filters

"What are filters while reading passages?" I asked.

"The filters I discussed earlier were more of retarders. Those were in another context. The filters which I am going to discuss now mean refining information. When you read passages, you require some filtering, you may not be able to process them all. In fact, doing so, you may get confused. Based on your interests, you may be attracted to passages having information about say, civil engineering, computer science, business insights, etc. But sometimes, you also need to process the information specific to only one field, say, in your case, textiles. Now, you may either go over only the textile related passages or you may go through each and every type of passage showing attentiveness and interest only in those passages which are related to textiles," he said.

"So, how can I filter the passages?" I asked.

"You don't need to do something special. You just need to keep in mind that you have to get textile related information and concentrate more on those topics. And even later, whenever you have doubts regarding textiles, you go only to those passages related to it, to find your answers, and not through each and every passage you went through the first time. Remember, although you may concentrate only on textile related passages, you should go through the other ones too, to help you reach 'A'. I told you earlier that there may be many things and fields related to textiles (like nanotechnology). So you never know, going through what you may find your 'A'. Filtering is important so that you have in view what you are looking for, but you cannot be sure to discard certain information/passage without going through it. You filter, while you read, and gather what you need. It's like you go through the newspaper, but keep an eye open to count the number of deaths, as you are especially looking for that," he said.

"So, if I am able to process lots of passages it means it's very good for me. Basically, I only need to be an expert at getting the knowledge and processing it fast. And by doing so I will be quickly moving towards my 'A'," I said.

"No, having lots of knowledge or passages is not a solution. In fact, reading so much may even be a hindrance when you are not able to understand each and everything. And having only the right passages is also tough, as you really need to be a top expert in the field, which may only come through years of experience. Getting the knowledge and being sure that what you have got is sufficient is also very important. Some of your friends would be experts in getting knowledge from the syllabus books. They easily gather the information and get goods marks. It's an important art, although not the only one you need to move forward on your way. But if you are not an expert at it, you really have to be. In fact, this is not limited to the syllabus books, but anything you think could be of importance. You must have heard many of your friends say that they wish to read a particular book, but they are unable to do so, maybe because it's too big, or they are unable to decide if it's worth a read or not and are afraid to waste their time over it. This is something you ought to manage. You have to skim through, gather what you can, and be able to decide if it's worth it, and do it quickly," he said.

Sources of Passages

"What are the common sources of passages? I mean, where should I look for these? What comes to my mind are:

1. Books
2. Magazines
3. Internet
4. Professors

"I said.

"You know, earlier getting the required information in the concise form of passages was really difficult. People used to brainstorm themselves, and with others collectively, read so many books, to come out with the required passages. Many times the texts did not even conclude. But today, except for books, everything else will help you get to 'A'. All these things can be used even for leisure, but they can help you reach 'A'," he said.

By Syllabus Books

Syllabus books have a lot of information about a particular field. These are much helpful when someone needs details and an in-depth study, not at the point when one is not clear about his/her goals. Although you can get 'A' through some parts of the book, especially the illustrations and the end results.

Facts related to books

1. The students studying most of the time are not considered to be brilliant. Getting a lot of knowledge is not the pain point but taking too much time to get it is.
2. If you are not a smart student, reading books may bore you. But if you can understand them well and quickly, and apply those things to solve problems easily while others are struggling to do the same, you will find reading books interesting and enjoy them too.
3. Most syllabus books are not proficient in telling you about the real life problems, or about the obstacles that hindered the progress while solving those problems. They mostly talk about the theory, proving and explaining it.

By Magazines/App

Magazines are a good way to get 'A'. There a lot of magazines out there through which one can get 'A'. Just a decade ago we did not have much free access to these but now, as the world goes digital, we have an access to a wide variety of magazines available at the tap of our hand through digital media, websites, and apps. All you need to do is find the ones that interest you and tap on subscribe. Thereon, you'll get all the emails, newsletters, magazines, articles, etc. right on your phone or your computer.

Syllabus books won't help much in getting ideas but are very helpful in working on the ideas, once you've found them.

At present, these modes are used by quite a lot of people, but there many who still use the old and conventional ways. Even today they prefer getting the topics from teachers or professors rather than using their self-observation. Consulting teachers and professors is not bad but blindly choosing the topic which they have in mind might not work out well for you. It may even have limitations, some specific to you, like – not having an interest in that area or topic, etc. So it's good to be aware and alert, and explore around to find your topic, no matter it's from magazines, apps or your mentors.

By Internet/Google

Just Googling around for topics, ideas, words, etc. may be useful but not always. You need to be smart at gathering the relevant information from Google.

In the blank space on Google, you can put any noun, verb, or even a complete topic, just any word or a set of words, and you will get a thousand links related to that. Each link tells about one of those thousands of methods through which you can find a problem and 'A'. The problem is not getting the links but finding the right one. You may not get your 'A' by reading the first link or the first passage you come across. You may need to go through quite a lot of those to get to your 'A'. Whatever you have in your mind, just put it on Google and right there, in a matter of milliseconds, thousands of links will be hurled at you.

At times, getting an 'A' is easy, getting a workable idea about it is tough, and practically finding ways to work on that idea, or so to say the solution, is the toughest and generally requires a long-term investment of time and resources. Here are a few examples of trying to search for a problem to solve:

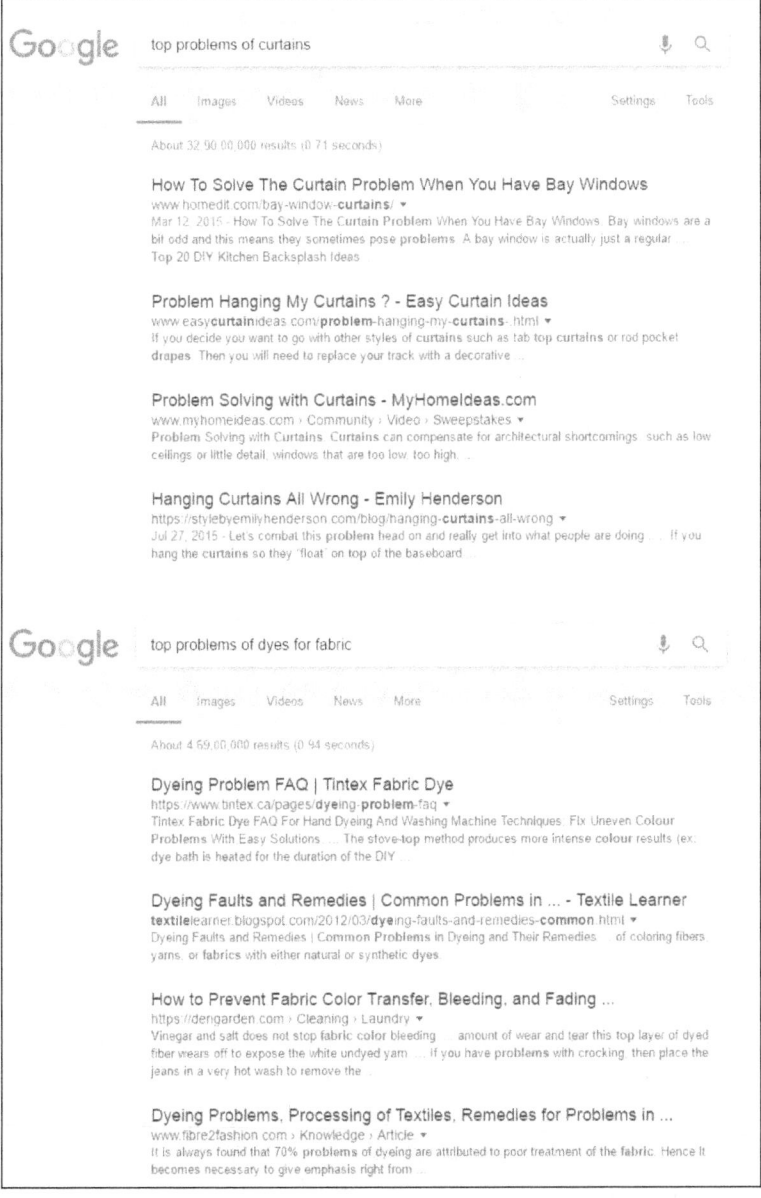

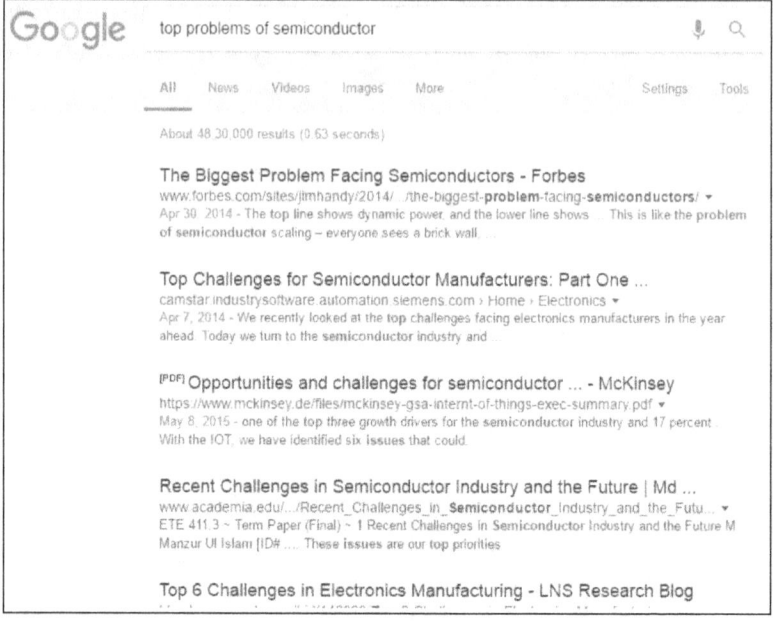

In fact, the word 'problem' in the above examples can be replaced by 'challenge', 'limitation', 'requirement' etc.

By Professor/Renowned Person

Every scientific person who has done something remarkable in science or tried his/her best would have

- Something which he/she hasn't solved yet.
- An interesting topic but not enough time to explore that.
- Some unexplained topics.

If you go through the lives of some major scientists, even some noble prize winners, they were motivated by their mentor professors. Many professors and scientists have lots of unexplored things and if you can get to know them you can have a substantial 'A' working on which you may come up with a breakthrough.

It is not only about professors, it could be any thinker. In fact, he/she may be helpful for you at the various stages of innovation - 'A', 'B', 'C', or 'D'.

"But in my college, no professor has discussed any such thing till now, why? I don't think they have much potential or even try to brainstorm or think of the problems, so how can I get help from them?" I asked.

"Who do you think is the most useless person for you to give you 'A'?" he asked.

"A friend of mine," I replied as I chuckled remembering him.

"Hmmm... Mark my words – No one can be useless. It may sound philosophical, but some of the things which your professor may be able to tell you, even the MIT professor may not be able to convey to you, although he/she may have much more knowledge to impart, but there would always be things specific to your environment, to your area, to your surroundings, which someone from there can explain best, no matter how good or intelligent another person may be in another part of the world. Even your friend, he may be able to tell you a few things about yourself which your teachers or even your parents may not be able to tell, because of the unique relationship you have with him," he explained.

"You know, once I asked a professor, who was lecturing us on a subject, about some innovative ideas. What he explained seemed interesting at the beginning, but soon that spark did not catch up. I think in the whole of India the professors of average colleges and universities of engineering, arts, etc. lack what it takes to ignite that spark," I said.

"That's your thinking, and I will answer it later," he said, "as we were discussing passages, let me continue on that first. Let me tell you what can be derived by a passage and what its uses are:

1. Problem
2. Facts
3. Various statement
4. Step solution
5. Whole solution

This list is not exhaustive. These are only a few examples of the things which can be derived from a passage. Some people have an extraordinary ability to process things and they may be able to extrapolate inferences from very basic passages and get quite a lot more from it than the average people. We all have our specific abilities to process information. Using our specific ways of thinking and optimizing those we can get astounding results.

By digging deep down into a passage one can find the problems that need to be solved. One should keep a keen eye towards the society in which he/she lives in, which can lead to great innovations. Things like - what could be done to bring the society to a better level, what can be done to make the place you live a better one, etc.

You may not restrict to the problems only in your area. Although we have some limitations like we may never be able to visit each and every place on earth and find the problems there, Internet or the digital media gives us passages from almost everywhere. Without even visiting, without even seeing or feeling things from those unknown areas, they give us a peek into the problems and situations prevalent there. That's the power of passages. Through the passage, you may be able to exchange your ideas and information by connecting to a person sitting in another corner of the world. Hence, a passage has a big probability to let you know things going around the world which need a solution or need to be brought to a better level.

The same goes for facts. Facts are those statements that have been agreed upon and marked true or proven. But we don't go proving each and every statement in our life. We don't live our lives only on proven statements, we do have quite a lot of assumptions. We are not perfect, so our assumptions may not always be right. At times we assume things based on inferences from other available information, facts, or proofs. But ultimately, these assumptions need to be proved either right or wrong. Once done, they too become facts. Hence, there are a countless number of facts, and again, it would be next to impossible to go through and know each and every fact in the world. Each fact may have been a breakthrough to solve a problem, confirmed or wronged an assumption or a statement, or may have become the basis of a new assumption. Facts too could help bringing things to the next level, or prove certain points. Statements are observations in a few lines. There may be proven and unproven/unverified/ambiguous statements. These are detailed in statement section. By looking at a statement, someone may get an idea to start working on or could find something which itself is an idea. Verifying a statement may be a breakthrough too.

One may be an expert at one or a few things, but certainly not at each and everything. Especially the average students in a class, they have so many flaws to take care of. Just like taking help from friends while solving a problem, one may get a solution, midway to your idea through passages. But the medium changes from verbal to passage and the person from friend to strangers. Using others' knowledge, some smart people can even get the whole solution to their problems."

"What are future possibilities of the passages?" I asked.

"There are lots of opportunities in this. People can be connected more with their ideas, and this can be more innovative. Group sharing of knowledge can make it much more helpful to each other.

In my opinion, even a twelfth-grade student can make a passage which may be helpful to a Ph.D. scholar while some problems of the graduate student can be solved by the Ph.D. scholar. So, mutually exchanging their ideas and experiences, they can help each other. Even at present, people use this technique already, as I mentioned earlier.

Another advantage of the passage is to communicate the ideas of one city to another, one state to another, and one country to another. Doing so, a broad chain of people may be focused on a single problem and the probability of solving it increases many folds.

Now you may wonder why anyone would want to share ideas publically for the fear of being copied and someone else coming up with a solution before him/her. Because we know that giving and sharing knowledge always increases your own knowledge too. Yes, there is a possibility of being copied, but there is also a possibility of building a collaboration with the best minds in the world and solving the problem, coming up with an innovation much faster, and with a better solution, than working on it alone. If you are sincerely working towards the betterment and getting a breakthrough, the pros of knowledge exchange are much more than its petty cons.

Below are the sources that hold the key to the future of passages. Some of these have already started ramping up and building passage resources for themselves and others:

1. College/University
2. Individual
3. Research Institute
4. Companies
5. Employees
6. Scientific novels

There are millions of passages having the possibility of the future invention, innovation, and business.

Colleges/universities are the places where many of the passages come into existence. These may also be the most creative. Students, professors, and research scholars are responsible for the creation of the passages, and they are also good at processing the currently available ones. The environment where the students and faculty are both onboard to prepare these knowledge artifacts and creative things with the faculty on one side bringing things to speed with, maybe, the traditional methods while the students can bring new and creative ideas through the newer upbeat methods, the output can be quick breakthroughs, breaking through the myths and rules of the past.

As an individual, I have found even some people of much higher age to be very creative. Once I found an old person talking about a manufacturing process of plastic case for the honeycomb. He told it with much vigor. Such people have so much to say, and their thoughts move way faster than they can speak, hence, they cannot put forward everything in one talk. So, it would be great if they can convert their thoughts, observations, and ideas into passages, which can even benefit others in finding their 'A' or a solution to their problems.

Research institutes are unique. They always have some ongoing research, and they are one of the best to be able to come up with useful, knowledgeable passages. These organizations can have their own 'A' and give 'A' to others too.

Companies working on creating things or doing various businesses can be a good source of passages. Through their experience in the business, and their constant need to grow and expand, they keep finding ways to streamline things, to do them in a better way, and to bring about things which can be beneficial for the world, so that they can sell them to the people. Documenting such things can be very useful and aid them, as well as others on the way to innovation. Employees are part of the companies, and the ones fulfilling the needs of the company. So ultimately, the employees will be the ones producing these passages as part of the company experiences and business. What kind of passages may come out vary from employee to employee – the higher management may be more focused on the business end, while a junior employee may be more focused on the technical aspects of the working or a solution.

Scientific Novels are great thought provoking, creative, imaginative books. They generally point our way to the future. They pave a way for those who would like to dare to accomplish that what has not yet been done. They are great at providing 'A', ideas, theories, suggestions on which no one yet has worked upon. Taking ideas from them may sound crazy, but then wasn't going to space and exploring planets just an idea before some people worked on it? It was sci-fi, it was the future, but now, so many missions have been sent to space."

Passage-1

Textile recycling innovation challenges clothing industry

There are many methods to recycle the textile products. Textile recycling is the process through which the rejected clothing and other textile materials are recovered for reuse or recovering of the material. Usually, the textile recycling involves donation, collection, sorting, and processing. The global textile industry has evolved into a $1 trillion business. Over 80 billion garments are produced annually. It is worth noting that the rate of textile recovery is still only 15%. While natural fibers consume a lot of time, space, labor, water, electricity, etc. resources, many of which are rendered useless just after a few uses, synthetic fibers have are not designed for recycling and are harmful to the environment while in production as well as when decomposed.

If the qualities of clothing are good, they are sorted and categorized by color, size, and quality. After that, they are prepared in the form of bales. A bale is a compressed form, which is easy to transport and takes less space for storage. The process not only creates jobs but also the apparel can be used again giving more value for the money and resources spent. The only drawback of this method to reuse the apparel is that the value of the apparel, along with the shine and luster of the fabric decreases. Once the color of the fabric fades it does not seem attractive. In another method of recycling the fibers are recovered from the materials and then converted into industrial wiping cloths and other items.

If the material is made of synthetic then they are recycled in a different manner, in fact, they are never used as is. First, they are filtered to remove the unwanted materials like buttons or metallic components. Then they are recycled into polymer chips. These polymer chips are again used to make fibers or other materials.

In India, the recycling of textile material is a little bit different. There are small scale industries to work on the second hand imported clothing and create a wide range of products. The products may be yarn, blankets, doormats, mattresses, and bed linen. Some pieces of cloth are cut down in square and rectangle piece and they are used in making home cleaning and industrial wipes. As there are a variety of fibers so the recycling practice is different. Cotton, wool, acrylic, polyester, silk, nylon etc. are the most common fibers. For recycling of wool and acrylic waste, Panipat the world's largest textile recycling hub produces 'shoddy' wool yarn from used winter clothing. They are produced in yarns, blanket, felt products. The business of using recycled acrylic and woolen threads for blanket manufacturing has annual revenues of up to 1000 crores in Panipat alone.

The recycling of textiles has great potential for innovation and creating more value from the fibers. Most recycled textile materials last only the first recycling. The second, third, and more stages of recycling hardly take place. Many apparels can be recycled to the same material even for the second and third recycling.

Passage-2

Here is a passage which a student, Archit Ojha, of NIT Raipur saw as an opportunity

A major challenge that I see in a biologically investigative environment in the developing countries trying to find the point of freezing/stunning of an animal, being calculated manually. The response of an animal in conditions of the fear experiment is recorded and the time frame of its stunning/freezing due to fear is done by us still by watching hours and hours of those videos. We are generally good at identifying the difference between an animal just sniffing or reacting to fear.

As a computer science enthusiast, if one could develop an automated alternative to it, you are in for a good opportunity as an entrepreneur.

Passage-3

Smart Textile

Smart textiles are also known as E-Textiles. These have some more attributes in comparison to the ordinary textiles. These are also known as smart fabrics, electronic textiles etc. These have some digital components embedded in them. E-textiles provide more value, functions, and features to the textiles. The latest technology is more suitable for them. How wonderful it is to be able to embed any attribute to textiles. These are gaining popularity because of the features they can provide about telling more about our body, keeping track, and monitoring our health, along with providing comfort.

There are two types of smart textiles:

1. *Aesthetic*
2. *Performance*

Aesthetic textiles are made from fabrics that can change properties, like changing color. They get energy from various resources like vibration, heat, sound, or may be small rechargeable batteries etched into the fabric itself.

Performance smart textiles are those which help perform things which our body cannot. They include extreme sports, avoiding radiation, military application etc. including applications that can monitor our body there are huge possibilities for performance smart textiles.

For research point of view there are huge opportunities in both aesthetic and performance smart textiles but commercializing may be tough. It would be great if someone commercializes smart textiles which may be useful in our everyday life and at lower cost and complexity, for example, an entrepreneur who wishes to combine smart textiles and party wear may have a huge success. The aesthetic properties in smart textiles can easily be changed so it will attract people for party wear. Also, as these textiles are customizable with respect to the features, people can easily opt for what all properties they need and can decide how much they would like to spend. Being a party wear, it may become a trendsetter, and popularity may not be a problem thereon, demand will automatically grow.

Passage-4

Indian farmers face a lot of problems. Recent news of the suicide of farmers is a major concern for India. Despite having a fertile land they face lots of problems because the land just being fertile is not enough. The major problems faced by them are as follows:

India has a very large population and even today a large amount of population depends on agriculture. The population is very dense even in the villages due to which the farmers only have small land holdings. This is not the end of the problems, the small lands are fragmented which creates even more complications. This problem is mostly seen in the states like Kerala, Uttar Pradesh, West Bengal, and Bihar, where the average size of land holding is even less than one hectare. Here, there is a wide gap between small, medium, and big farmers, with respect to the land they hold. As land is fragmented it causes problems like irrigation, crop security, doing related activities on time, unavailability of agriculture-related machines, etc. The major technologies in machines which come related to agriculture are mostly for large land holdings. For example, a small farmer cannot even afford a harvester.

The quality of seeds is one of the major foundations behind the crop yield. As the technology increases, the quality of seed is also increasing but the accessibility of seeds to medium and small farmers is still a challenge. As better quality seeds cost more, hence, they are out of reach of the small farmers. Even if the seeds are accessible to them they lack the knowledge to use them optimally. Many with traditional mindsets are even skeptical of buying these better quality seeds because they are processed and have enhanced abilities to bear the crop.

Indian soil has been exhausted of many nutrients due to the growing of crops over thousands of years without caring much. So, manures and fertilizers play a big role in getting a high yield. But the problem is the lack of knowledge among the farmers. There are certain crops which need to be grown in cycles, not doing so, due to lack of knowledge, or high demands, is causing more exhaustion to the fertility of the land. If fertilizers are applied, it can bring 70% growth in agriculture production. Cow dung is one of the best manures but it is also used as a kitchen fuel, which has complicated the problem. At present, 650 million tons and 160 lakh tons compost have potential to fertilize the rural and urban agricultural lands, but they are not fully/optimally utilized. It can actually solve two problems - disposal of waste and fertilize the soil.

India is one of the top irrigated countries in the world. Yet only one-third of the total crop is irrigated. Monsoon is not regular and insufficient to fulfill all needs.

Although the large-scale mechanization has been done yet the middle and small farmers still operate a major part of their cultivation by hand using conventional tools. No machines are used for ploughing, harvesting, weeding, pruning, threshing, transporting, etc. of the crop. This results in more hard work and less output. There is a huge opportunity for innovations in these processes.

Agriculture marketing is in a bad shape in rural areas. One reason may be small farmers. Control of traders and middlemen on the crops have ruined the margins of small and medium farmers. Farmers who borrow money from these traders and middlemen are forced to give their crop at dirt cheap prices. In the case of any loss, it has to be borne by the farmers while any extra margin is taken by the traders and the middlemen.

The inadequate storage facility is another major reason behind the poor condition of the farmers. After harvesting, the small and medium farmers are forced to sell their crop as soon as possible, due to lack of proper storage, or the costs involved in using rented storage areas. At this time, the crops are bought at very cheap prices. Due to inadequate storage facilities, the prices fluctuate very much and too frequently causing losses to farmers, as well as the end buyers. It only profits smart traders and middlemen.

Analysis

Analysis can give an idea to work upon. When you analyze people, places, surroundings, objects, etc. you get an opportunity to get your 'A' to work upon. It is not a new method. Scientist, innovators, businessman, inventors, have already been using it. Once they are in equilibrium with the experience of analyzing and working on things, they come out with various successful solutions. You know Edison had over a thousand patents because he was very good at analyzing things and working on them.

Slowly, as we grow, we somewhere start accepting things as they are. We start taking them for granted. We stop questioning them to be problems. Sometimes we also think about them, but they don't get solved because we never questioned them when we could have solved them. We see lots of problems every day which we don't solve. A child sees lots of problems but he can't solve as he is too young, as people get older they take everything for granted and don't question. But some of the people have questions and they find answers and solve problems. They are scientists, innovators, inventors, business people, entrepreneurs, etc.

Analyzing people can be much more interesting than you think. You may not like reading books but this is something you will enjoy. Analyzing people and connecting it with science and its abilities is more important than just having lots of knowledge.

It will be a great pleasure for you when you find any solution to the problems of the people after analyzing them.

Let me tell you a story. When Jene Chen visited India she noticed a lady named Savita who gave birth her daughter, Rani. Savita took her baby to a nearby clinic where the doctor referred her to the hospital which was nearly 4 hours away. She was unable to take the baby to the hospital due to which her baby died. Shaken by this story Jene Chen and her team started working on the problem.

Jene Chen invented a baby incubator which costs less than 25 dollars, which is just 0.1% of the cost of a traditional incubator which costs around 25000 dollars. Jene Chen looked over the requirement of the product in India. Throughout the world, nearly twenty million children are born prematurely. About four million of them die every year. But the bigger problem is that even those who survive have long-term health problems.

Pranav who did his diploma in HVAC (heating, ventilating and air conditioning) worked as a product manager for various companies for almost fourteen years. His wife says, "Initially Pranav's office used to be at home, so during the summer of 2010, his father pulled him up for the heavy electricity bill. So he thought of an idea and tried fitting a compressor into a cooler. Later he kept working and optimizing it. Once he was satisfied with the result, he got his technology patented.

His technology uses only 250 watts of electricity and gives sufficient cooling effect. He compromised a little on the lowered temperature and humidity, leading to the reduced wattage of the air conditioning device named 'Vaayu'.

"Did they complete all these things so easily, as it seems from what you told?" I asked.

"No, what I told you in just a few lines actually took many years to complete, from getting the idea to completing it," he said.

"But tell me one thing, why my analysis would matter when billions of people have been born till now and many of them would have felt the same problem. So many of them would

have the same 'A' what I have. How can things be easy for me?"
I asked.

"First of all, all people would not face all the problems of the
world, and in the same way. Hence, their 'A' may not be exactly
the same. Even those who have the same 'A' may not have the
same 'B' or the ease of access to 'B' through the modern means.
Even those who have the 'A' and ease of access to 'B' would not
have the same technologies available for completing them. A
gap of even a few years can be a reason for success to a solution
or to get a solution. Before the arrival of YouTube, there was
a website shareyourworld.com which was quite similar to
YouTube but it failed in 2001 because of various issues like
internet speed," he said.

"Every moment nature is giving you a new opportunity to
explore and analyze it. You may find lots of opportunities but
getting the opportunity which can be solved by you is important.
I'll give you my analysis," he continued.

"In India, mostly ladies have the responsibility of making
food. This custom is quite old. Ladies of the past did not go to
work, hence, they had lots of time to make food and they did it
very well. But today, women are part of the work in all walks
of life. They work shoulder to shoulder with men and many
women do not have a preference or inborn liking towards
preparing food. But still, as it is customary here that women
are responsible for preparing food, they are bound to do so,
they may like it or not. There could be many solutions to this
problem. Pranoti Nagarkar Israni found a solution for this. She
invented a machine which could prepare rotis automatically and
named it, Rotimatic. You just need to feed it with Wheat, water,
and oil, and it gives you fresh rotis. This is the first invention of
its kind," he said.

"Isn't it funny, automatic roti maker?" I laughed.

"It seems funny because we are not conditioned to think
beyond the boundaries and also because it doesn't look like it
can serve the purpose of people. But will you believe, it does,
and the people who have just started using it are really happy.

You discard some ideas or don't take them seriously because you are not mature enough, and generally overrate or underrate an idea. It looks either too easy or overly hard to accomplish to make it real," he said.

I got silent and pondered over what he just said. These were not mere words in the air, this was experience talking. If I connect myself to these stories and how I felt about them, his words were just so true. Every word he said had a great meaning. What he said was not only related to 'A' and getting its solution but a general philosophy about getting ideas, about invention, innovation, business, etc. And also how these things are connected to each other.

"Please tell me more about analysis," I asked.

"Business is the most used way of serving people. By doing business you earn money for yourself. There are many people who even give their technologies or platforms for free. The first way of doing business is just providing the already available goods and services at places where they are currently unavailable or by buying franchises like opening another Dominos outlet. If you don't want to be very creative, this can work out well. You just have to look for such business idea which is already existing and has much potential in the specific area. It may have its limitations, especially if you are the creative types.

Another way could be, customizing an existing business idea to best fit the needs of the people where you are providing your goods and services. In such a situation, you do something innovative in your business. This is the most popular way of doing business these days.

The third type could be, you invent something and bring it to the market. This may take quite a long time and may require a good amount of R&D. The idea may be from a single person, but finally, when the product launches in the market, it's a group effort. I think I'm diving deep into this topic. There are many books and theories that can explain these things very well if you wish to go in further detail.

When you analyze people and their problems, you tend to get a set of requirements which can lead to innovative solutions. By analyzing things in this way you can also invent something, but it all depends upon your thinking and your way of handling 'A' which will determine if you would come up with an innovative solution or something more like an invention.

If you concentrate on observing data, scientific results, their flaws, and possibilities, you may come up with something great which can help in giving something revolutionary to science. Such a breakthrough may not be helpful to the people right then but it could help them in due course of time. Noble prize winners are a great example for this."

"So analyzing does not mean that mere uninteresting word you hear like simply inspecting or monitoring something. It is much more than that," I said.

"Definitely, it's about observing the places, people, science, etc. If you observe these things you are most probable to find your 'A'. You may have some friends who study a lot. But if they are not observing these things they may end up not using their knowledge and will be left feeling frustrated," he said.

I looked at my watch and said, "Ok Robin, I have to go to the market with a friend. At night, I will try to recapitulate whatever we have discussed and will then discuss with you," I said.

* * *

"Last night I thought a lot and stumbled upon an observation which I found interesting. But after some time I had nothing to think, not even new topics," I said.

"One cannot get good at observation in one night. By the way, what was your observation about?" he asked.

"Getting up early in the morning is one tough thing. I think if anyone makes such an alarm which will not stop until it ensures I have woken up no matter what, it will be a great product. But I think such alarms would already be there," I said.

98

"Although alarms do exist yet you can make some futuristic alarms. The alarms of the present do not use any mechanism which complies with an individual's mind. I have no clue how it can be built but I know that there is chance to build if you remember the equation

$$Z = Y - X$$

Here Z is the resulting value for a person. Y is all the positive value provided by the product for the person while X is all the negative value. For example, you have made a machine, let's assume a robot, which can do some of the tasks for which you currently take the help of a paid helper. Now, if the complexity of handling the device is much more than the complexity of actually getting it done by the helper, the device will be useless. Earlier computers were not suitable for an ordinary person because of the cost and complexity involved in purchasing and handling them. But now, computers have become a part of the ordinary human because the value 'Y' increased and the negatives 'X' decreased. That's why we are now using them extensively. You may find lots of patents which could never be commercialized because 'Y' was less and 'X' was more. If you get an answer, a solution or an idea for your 'A' you should always think of how 'Y' can be increased and how 'X' can be decreased," he said.

"You said you did not get any topics to analyze. I am going to tell you how to analyze things from today and you will never again say that you have no topics to analyze. Below is a small list of what kinds of analysis you can do. You can even find your own ways and add to the list.

1. People based analysis
2. Product based analysis
3. Service based analysis
4. Activity based analysis
5. Technology based analysis
6. Patent based analysis
7. History based analysis

People based analysis

If you go through the lives of many scientists, business people, inventors, and innovators, you will find that 'people based' analysis is one of the most extensively used tool for innovations and inventions, where they have affected the lives of billions of people. And why not, it's based on the needs and betterment of the people.

Examples of people are students, adults, children, scientist, business person, old people, etc.

By considering any one or more of these categories, you can come up with the required 'A'.

Example-1 Smart bottles - students may be using water bottles while studying. Now these bottles can be modified to have a little useful technology right in the bottle mold, which could give some useful information or tips, and ensure that students remain hydrated. It may give information like how much water they have drunk, and how much more they should, etc.

Example-2 Students use alarms to wake up in the morning. As discussed in an example earlier, some smart alarms can be made analyzing the student mind and how it works, so that it is more efficient, and can be customized and help each person in a specific way.

Example-3 Analysing people while making rotis. Although roti maker is now available in the market, but it's the first version, there may be many betterments required in it, and to bring it closer to how we manually make rotis, again we need to analyze people while they are making them.

Example-4 A child noticed her mother had to spread washed wheat on the roof. It was a tedious task in the hot sun, and it took quite a lot of time. So she thought of making such a device which could help her spread the washed wheat much more quickly, spending very less time outside under the hot sun.

In people analysis, the word 'people' is given the maximum weightage. You drive yourself because of the people, and their requirement.

Product based analysis

Take a fresh, unique, out of the box product and look where it can be applied. As you are a textile engineer, every year there are some new products which are quite new to the world and they have much more possibility to pick up popularity over the world. **Example-1** Air conditioned mattress made by Gentherm are in their first version. They can be a somewhat modified and popularized even among tropical and sub-tropical countries.

"Is it necessary to fill each and every gap or each and every analysis?" I asked.

"No, it's just given to you so that you know what the possibilities are. Having just two may be sufficient for a breakthrough and having all also may not make your idea strong," he said and asked, "Did you ever analyze people related to textiles?"

"I never realized there could be such a direction, and never tried to think in such terms till now. All we do is just swallowing syllabus before the night of the exam. Do you think a student like me would do things like analyzing people?" I asked.

"Why not? As I've repeatedly explained to you that when you are asked to be engaged in things which you don't like, then it's better to analyze something there than just sitting and feeling frustrated.

Try to be in all types of environments. Analyzing things is a very easy way to make your time productive. If you live in one place and then you go to another, even then you start noticing the differences between those places. You do it subconsciously already, you just need to do it consciously now. Go and read books and find out how the life was before the invention of a particular thing like electricity, the telephone, etc. Try and understand the thinking and concepts of people before and after certain inventions.

Analyzing things is a continuous and everlasting process. From the very early civilizations, people used their skills of analysis to find something, understand their needs, and fulfill them.

Analyzing people and finding the notion what they wish for or what could make their lives even a little bit better falls under people analysis. We all wish to get ourselves at a better place from where we started. There has already been something which can improve one's life to a great extent. Science is advancing to greater heights but the 'A' remains at the same place until someone makes the connection between them. This is the way people start serving others. There has always been a gap between an advancement of science and using it to serve people. This gap sometimes is too big and can last even a decade or a century. So the analysis of this advancement/products to bring them to the people or make them better so that they can serve people in some way comes under product analysis.

Some requirements of people living in the 18th century or even before could be:

1. An easy way of commutation.
2. Easy purchasing system.
3. The requirement of a good health system.

These are just a few things which were required at that time. These are those requirements about which people would talk about. Children have always been wondering about having such a mat on which they could ride and go anywhere they want. There have been cartoons on this. There are a lot of things which people used to just think and wonder at that time, but those are real today. They had no expectation of actually getting them or making them real, but the innovative people used these imaginations and came out with such things.

The requirements are what people need. Some of them can be fulfilled by current technologies while some cannot be. Most of the technologies do not apply directly to fulfill the needs, they are combined with the other technologies and concepts to bring about the fulfillment. Sometimes creating these combinations require much more hard work than it took to invent them. A person who has invented the technology may not be able to guess all the possibilities of its application.

If one looks at a location, he/she may come with the business idea. Many people can challenge me saying that those who come up with business solutions do not necessarily need to be inspired by the location, they also get inspired by people. I'd like to reply that they are mainly inspired by innovations." Inventions are more to do with the needs of the people. A business running well or not depends more on the place where it is set up. Example, Dominos – If it's placed near a nice upbeat area it could work, but if it's located in a remote village, will it work?

Now go and see around and try to find out any problems you or anyone around may be facing," he said.

After returning to my friend, we sat on a bench in the park discussing our college. My mind was still racing with the thoughts Robin had explained me and looks like my analysis mode was on. I saw a girl walking with her friend on the walking track. I kept staring when my friend elbowed me and said, "Hey buddy! Stop staring at girls," I replied, "I'm not staring, am analyzing what problems that girl could be facing with her clothing."

He laughed and said, "Listen bro, firstly, she is a girl, so even if she would have a problem you are least likely to find that out. Secondly, even if you find one, either you should have much experience or be a great analyzer to do something about it."

I thought I should list down whatever analysis I do. So I took out a pen and paper and started writing down my analysis.

1. Most of the times when I buy an apparel, it fades after some time. I think many people would be facing this issue. Even the branded clothes I buy, many times they are discolored in some time.
2. We have many clothes which we stop wearing due to this but the clothes do have their properties. I think recycling textiles has a good chance to get more value out of them.

Next day I went to Robin and told him about my idea.

"Oh wow. You did some analysis and were able to jot down two points! That's wonderful. When I started analyzing, I wasn't able to write anything for about a week," he said.

"So what idea did you get after one week?" I asked.

"That I'll tell you later. Now you go and try to find out some problems that may exist even though you may not face them. You may take the help of internet, magazines, or anything," he said

Next day I went to the college and read out many articles in a magazine. After some time I got a headache. I was just about to give up when I found an interesting article related to smart textiles in which something about illuminating textiles was explained.

"So, did you get any idea?" he asked.

"I didn't get much. I read many articles and found them boring which made me very tired. But when I was just about to give up I got an interesting article which was related to the illumination of textiles. Some scientists have been using special lights in clothes."

"What were the challenges mentioned in making it real?" he asked.

"Durability and increase in attraction," I replied

Here I am giving you some of my analysis. Going through these, you'll find that you actually know these problems exist but somehow did not notice them.

Analysis-1

Most students face something or the other in their lives. Some things are interesting, some are inspirational, some are funny, and some are tragic. Many of them have big expectations from their lives. Some are able to achieve those, some don't. Those who achieve their goals in life are an inspiration to others, while those who don't, have some important things to articulate to others which they learnt through their experiences. Students in hostels may have more experiences than day scholars. So, if anyone could record the experiences which could be useful for others, it could be great.

Analysis-2

Specialized bricks with a unique sticking property - Bricks can be put one over the other and made to stick without the need to expend money on plaster, putty paints, etc. Also, this unique property could be used to stick nonwoven wallpapers without glue. If this can be made commercially viable a lot of time, money, and effort can be saved.

Analysis-3

Once I analyzed that bringing more and more innovations and inventions and making people more and more comfortable right after birth, since childhood, may not be the best idea. If our ancestors would be living today to see the advancements we have made, they would be astounded, overwhelmed, and excited to see each and every development. But our generation, our children are not much excited or feel much about the new inventions or advancements; they are so used to them. I think one reason could be us providing them everything on a platter right from their childhood. In contrast, if you see the children from the village, they get excited when they visit the cities and first see these advanced things. What I see is that those who are born with all facilities, so to say with the silver spoon, don't much appreciate the advances human race is making.

The main point I want to mention is appreciating the difference. Although I'm not able to figure out exactly how, but see, when we see a person dying on the road we feel blessed being alive. When we see a bad dream and wake up, we feel blessed it was just a dream. Students keep complaining about facilities, but they don't appreciate what all they have already got.

The problem is, we take things for granted. Being alive, being able to do things, even being able to think about doing things, we are blessed, we are lucky that we can. We need to make the most of it, rather than taking it for granted. If we remember this each moment, we will utilize our time wisely and in a good way. So maybe, if there can be an app that conditions our mind to feel and stay blessed, it would be great.

Analysis-4

Nanotechnology is getting much attention these days. Once I saw that with the help of nanotechnology we can make such surfaces which won't even let a droplet of water stick to it. You may see some T-shirts, shoes, etc. using such stuff which has no effect of pouring water on it. Teflon is such a coating which is less sticky and water resistant. Nanotechnology is advancing to its peak. The possible applications of nanotechnology are still being explored. The non-sticking property of nano-coating materials may bring revolutionary changes to the apparel and footwear industry. You may even use this for preparing the dough.

Analysis-5

Every year I notice some of the clothes getting wasted even though they are not torn from any place. It's just because they are faded. Whenever I see this I feel so much of the earth's resources getting wasted just because it was not dyed properly. It may be good for the companies because people need to buy more apparels but as a customer and someone who cares about earth and environment, I get concerned. This must not be ignored and something should be done about it.

So there is a chance if a company can make apparels with a good dye that they are not faded, it would be great. Recycling of materials will also increase with the increase in the quality of apparels. In fact, with the good designing of apparels, if they can be made such that they are not torn, or even if they are, the part of the fiber/cloth can be replaced. This way, the life of an apparel can become endless. This would be revolutionary in the textile industry.

Analysis-6

Creative works attract people from all walks of life from children to adults. Creativity may not always be in physical form or with physical things. Even an app can be very creative, and I know you like this platform. So, you could make a creative app for the interior decoration of a house. I know there would be millions of things to do in this, but step by step, slowly and slowly, you can keep adding things to it. There is no lack of variety, it's just, taking that variety to the tap of your fingers. One may say that it is not the task of a textile engineer but of a civil engineer. It may be, but you are not actually doing it, you are providing a facility, a platform for house decoration using the products that are already available in the market. In fact, those companies, selling these products will be happy to promote their products through your app, as they will be getting more business. You could add budget options, and with that bring more and more people onboard to use your app. People may like such an app where they can make their dream home and get the best views right from the tap of their fingers.

Analysis-7

'Khoya' is one of the most liked sweet in South Asia. But manufacturing it is quite a tedious task. It is time-consuming and requires a lot of resources. The labor charge also increases its cost. For removing such tedious work someone may make a machine or a suitable pot or vessel which could avoid the labor. The machine can be as simple as that costs just a few thousand rupees while it may be as costly as lakhs of rupees, depending upon if it is being made for households or factories. If it is made for home use, I think it will be very popular.

Analysis-8

Labor and Mistry are those who build the house. There are lots of technologies for large constructions but at the lower level i.e. while making small 1/2/3 BHK houses or rooms, people rely on manual labor. These workers perform many tasks which are manual and time-consuming, like checking the level with respect to the ground after placing each brick. If some small machine can be built which is less costly, and can aid them with this, the process will be much quicker, accurate, and efficient. A lot of time and effort will be saved, and the quality of construction is bound to improve.

Similarly, while preparing the roof of the house, some tedious manual processes are done, to take the required resources at the intended height, place them accurately, and fix them. Maybe some cheaper hydraulic systems can come up which can aid the construction of roofs for small houses. They may take only a little while to install and thereon, the construction of the roof can begin. It would also increase the accuracy of such tedious and complex construction, taking care of the inclination angles.

So, those firms who make the construction equipment have an opportunity to work out some innovative ways and improve the construction of smaller houses.

Analysis-9

Nowadays, the business of restaurants is booming. Every restaurant wants to show itself to be one of the best in the locality. For doing so they work very hard, but one thing which I think is still missing is the possibility of semi-automatic kitchens. These will not only reduce the burden of chef and his/her crew but also could keep the kitchen cleaner and tidier. It is the innovator's vision which could make things much easier for the chef as well as the owner of the restaurant, and the quality of food and service provided to the customer could reach a new level. Happy customers could lead to many folds growth.

For example, pots/vessels/utensils could be designed in such manner that they could be washed semi-automatically without much manual intervention. Raw materials which are required for making food like finely cut onions, potatoes, tomatoes, chilies etc.

could be done through large food processors. These could be cut at the beginning of the day and stored in a cold chamber near the cooking place. Even the dough could be prepared automatically. Individually some of these machines are available, but a complete set semi-automatic kitchen module or unit is not. There may be some effort in training the crew to use these machines, but once done, this would be more efficient leading to happier customers.

Analysis-10

Roving breakage at Simplex and ring frame is one of the most common incidents which takes place. These breakages are very hard to find, and it makes the shift officers much concerned. The problem is not the removal of these breakages but the identification of the reason behind them. One solution which I see may be installing high-speed cameras at various places. These cameras will be able to show everything in slow motion when the breakage takes place. One may work on it and be able to make a theory on the breaking of sliver and yarn.

Analysis-11

Once while going for a coaching class I found that I missed an important notebook. One more time such a thing happened. Then I thought why not have such a notebook which would be like an iPad or a Tab and I could retain everything into that. Its features should be same as of notebook. I don't want a distraction, so I don't want it to be an iPad or a tab, but just a simple notebook. It should cost below 10000 and there is a big market for it. Remember that it will require innovations.

Analysis-12

Having a mobile means having another mind near you. There are many people out there who know well how to tackle the problems our mind is facing. Not only people but there are some other methods to still your mind or improve your mental state. So any medium which could know and understand our mental state can help us a lot. For example, you may create something on the social media which could help people by knowing their mental state and connecting to the right people at the right time. Let us assume that someone is preparing for an exam, so, the social media can show him/her about the other people doing the same and how they are coping up with this. At such a time, showing how other people are enjoying themselves may not be the best idea, hence, knowing the state of the mind and providing a useful feed would be helpful.

Analysis-13

Cutting of crops is such a hectic and laborious task. In India, especially the small and medium farmers, even now do most of this work manually, by hand. This can be made easier by creating some smaller portable machines which may be of help in these small farms. A machine which could replicate and increase the efforts of human muscles and manual work. While working there are a lot of muscles which work simultaneously. We feel tired when our weak muscles start feeling tired. That is why we invented bicycle and we can travel much more distance now, expending much less energy, than on foot. In the same way, such machines can be made which could help a lot not only to ease the work but also give them a chance to earn more by cutting more crop in a day, making the whole process quicker and more efficient.

Statements

" Statements are those small deductions which help us have results instantly without going into long quests. They are similar to formulae and theorems. Knowingly or unknowingly, we are always using statements, and they play a big role in our lives. We all have some experiences throughout our lives. We remember our experiences as a summary and use them as statements thereon; we don't have to go through the same experience again and again. What I am telling you through my experience are statements. We use our own statements, statements of our ideals and beliefs, and also of others who we think are wise in their specific arenas. If I say, 'only work hard and you will be successful' you will not believe me because from your experience you know, only working hard may not be sufficient. Although you cannot prove it, but you believe in it from your personal experience, and that is what you can narrate to someone to explain that working hard alone may not be sufficient.

Theorems save us from those long methods of proving something which has already been established and has no necessity to be proved again and again. You take them as a base and come up with other higher, more complicated things. Proving them again is like re-inventing the wheel. It's done. Every time you create land-based vehicles, you simply use them. Besides saving time it requires lesser brainstorming, preventing

111

you from exhaustion, and making your life comfortable. It offers quick deduction points bringing stability to solutions.

In 1962, red LED was invented by N. Holonyak Jr. and S. F. Bevacqua. Then, in 1968 green LED was invented by R.A. Logan and his colleagues. At that time, there was a statement "if we could invent blue LED too, there could be various applications which can affect human lives to a great extent." This was the major inspiration behind the invention of the blue LED. It was an approved statement which led to more statements and deductions helping to bring about more inventions.

During the innovation process, one needs lots of assumptions so that you can concentrate on the important things. For example, for innovation, you also need to know about the consumer behavior. But no one can tell a proven behavior of the customer. The ways and methods of proving this may also be very different from a science practical or experiment. Proving these need complex explanations and extrapolations from the right set of data sets (people). Mostly, the mindset of a few applicable people is taken into consideration and surveys are done on them to find out how they would respond to such inventions or products. They are not the complete set of people who would be finally using the final products. Examples are taken such as - if out of 100 selected people, 20 people do not like the idea; the research states that 80 percent of the people liked the idea, hence it would be good. But this is a farfetched guess and in reality may not work like that, although, if the selected people were very close to how most applicable people in the world are, this research would be almost correct. So here, a lot depends on the selection criteria.

For example, most people say 'one should always speak the truth'. It's a philosophical thing, one cannot prove it. Similarly, 'one should not tell a lie' is another subjective statement and we cannot prove it. You may get examples in favor and against both the statements. There are lots of statements regarding the common purchaser and they are used widely in the field of business. Most entrepreneurs come up with new trends for consumer and they predict if customers will like them or not. At times they are right, but there are times when they are wrong.

Fischell's latest idea sounds like a science fiction, "I'm working on a method to remove all human pain, with no drugs or side effects, with just a ten-minute treatment," he says. "I know that sounds crazy, but I believe it's going to work." He has designed a device which you can fit on your lower back, knee or neck-wherever you experience chronic pain. It delivers targeted magnetic pulses. Using Faraday's law, the pulses turn into electrical current in the body. He believes this will destroy or confuse the electrical signals from the pain causing neurons to the brain.

Innovation processes typically require statements regarding two things, one is people while the other is science. Some statements are proven, while some are not.

The statements used are of three two types:

1. Proved statement.
2. Unproved statement.

Proved statements are those which have been tested/verified/validated successfully and they have been marked as true. Their chances of being wrong are nearly negligible. Basically, scientific statements are proved because they can be tested and verified e.g. theorems. Every time you try to prove them, you will get the exact same result

Examples:

1. Abel's theorem (mathematical analysis).
2. Abelian and Tauberian theorems (mathematical analysis).
3. Abel–Jacobi theorem (algebraic geometry).
4. Abel–Ruffini theorem (theory of equations, Galois theory).
5. Abhyankar–Moh theorem (algebraic geometry).
6. force = mass x acceleration.

Unproved statements are those which have not yet been proved or are so subjective or philosophical that they may not be proved. With respect to a situation or perspective, they may be right or wrong and have no global acclaim of being perfectly true. These statements are also needed. While giving statements about philosophy and the working of the mind, behavior patterns etc. where many complex scenarios arise, everything may not be proved.

Examples:

1. There is much scope in getting remarkable products related to nanotechnology.
2. If I keep reading books on the success stories of entrepreneurs, I can work as a consultant for others."

"How are statements different from ideas or quotes?" I asked.

He answered, "An idea is something which does not emphasize on specifics, it talks about a wider spectrum where something can be done and it may or may not work. While when you say a statement, you say it firmly emphasizing the point you want to make through it, as you believe it to be true. The quotes are said by others based on their experience and we may or may not take them seriously. We may be able to relate to some of them and find them inspirational, funny, romantic or entertaining, but they may not be a basis for the things we do."

"Yesterday, one of my professors was saying that nonwoven fibers have much scope in the future. He also presented some facts behind it," I added.

"You may call it a statement. He is your professor, if you believe in him, you may take it as a basis for your work. Also, when you listen to something from lots of people then you start believing in it. You heard your professor say this statement, now if some other day you also hear it from a business person, your belief in the statement will become stronger. So unproved statements work in this way. They start from somewhere and slowly pick up to become well-known statements.

Let's solve a problem you would have come across while preparing for the IIT exam.

Question 1. The displacement-time graph of a moving particle is shown below. The instantaneous velocity of the particle is negative at the point _____

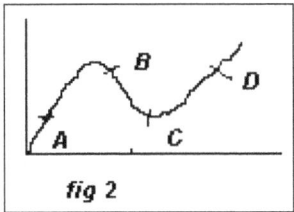

fig 2

You may have statements in all fields, even while solving physics or mathematics problems. To solve the problems related to the circle I used to remember the theorems and properties of circles which acted as my concepts. Some short tricks using which we could get answers quickly were also statements.

These were mere syllabus questions, but when you have to solve real life problems using the complex technical knowledge, you need have many statements which will help you sail through. They are like an emotional drive. You believe more in your own ideas than those of others until you get sufficient reasoning behind them, so do they need from you to believe in your ideas," he said.

"I have a close friend. We used to solve problems together and sometimes when he used to solve them before me, I felt jealous. I would ask him how he solved the problem so quickly and sometimes he would tell me short tricks or concepts which he had attained through much practice and experience but sometimes he won't tell me. I was no different to him, sometimes I told my tricks and sometimes I didn't," I chuckled.

"When you have a statement, you have a choice to use it or not. Basically, you tend to avoid situations of confusion so you select one statement and then you either prove it or disprove it. For example, when you are told a statement, 'nonwoven fibers have a great potential' and you choose to work on it, you choose it with full enthusiasm and put in your best. Now, after working, either you find that it indeed has good potential or you have collected some good amount of information and data which sees it otherwise, denoting not a good potential. When you have statements, your statements have the most chance of either supporting or contradicting others' statements, so to say, establishing them to be true or false," he said.

"Why it is necessary to mention statements? What are the advantages of writing them down?" I asked.

"If someone just comes and tells me something, would my mind accept that blindly? No. To convince me, he will have to use supporting statements. Now, if I believe in his statements, or if his statements are logically sound or have a valid base behind them that I am able to believe in them, then I will also believe in the point he was trying to make. I may even use that statement for my purposes thereon. But if his statements are vague and do not comply with my own set of thoughts and statements which I have established from my experience, the chances are, I will not believe in the point he is trying to make," he said.

Examples

Examples of statements for 'A'

1. Water has sufficient power to cool human body.
2. 10 watts is sufficient to cool down a room.
3. Buses can be cooled down at a lesser cost and the overall cooling in buses is higher than the normal vehicles.
4. We should be able to supplement energy instead of consuming it to bring down the temperature of the room.
5. The energy required for cooling is much less, only a few watts than what we actually spend.
6. At present we spend a lot of energy in cutting down crops.
7. A sweeper can clean much more area as compared to the present, in the time he/she spends cleaning.
8. Labor are ready to work to their full capacity if you give them Rs.1000/day.

9. It is possible to predict the speed of air outside just by the sound of the swaying trees.

10. The area of the field an Indian farmer has, he himself can crop the whole field.

11. Seeding is possible without cultivation.

12. For a crop, we consume much more water than it actually requires.

13. It is easier and there is more money in coming up with innovations in processes after the fabric is made in comparison to the innovations that could be done before the fabric is made.

14. Dehumidifying an environment requires very less energy.

15. At present, the cost of traveling to space is much higher than the actual cost in which this travel could be done.

16. It is quite possible to cool down the body at no cost even while working very hard in the sunshine.

17. Most of our mental needs can be fulfilled through the internet.

18. The concept of temperature transformer.

19. The temperature transformer can revolutionize getting energy from unconventional sources.

20. It may be possible to lower down the output temperature of the propulsion system.

21. Our bed can give us much more comfort than what it currently gives.

22. It is possible to make low energy consumption beds for villagers to give them some comfort in hot weather.

23. We can get a much better class environment in online classrooms compared to the physical classrooms.

24. Schools can be made self-sufficient in energy.

25. If you can make a surface which is very smooth and has good strength then you can make floor tiles with it.

26. If a food item is tasty and easy to preserve, it can be sold.

27. If you can make a two-minute tester of bacteria then it can support a million dollar business.

28. People pay more money while traveling.

29. If an item is somewhat tasty, gives good nourishment, acts as a supplement to food and can be preserved then you have a good opportunity to create a business around that.
30. Advertising can be made so interesting that people themselves will require it and would love to pay for it.
31. Any surface which appears in front of a human face can be used for advertising.
32. If one can make a low-cost machine for agriculture which could be operated manually, by the solar cell, or is battery operated then it can help a lot of farmers.
33. Stems of wheat and rice can be used to make low-cost mattresses for the winter season. All those materials which have low fiber quality can be used in making mattresses. And this can be done through the nonwoven process. As these are cellulosic materials so their moisture regain will also be high.
34. Automatic color making mechanisms for painters can be made and it can help lots of painters.
35. A glass panel which can be made completely opaque or transparent as and when desired can have a great market. This can be done using Liquid Crystals.
36. A re-dyeable fabric can change the world of the apparel industry.
37. A low-cost compressor operated by concentrated solar energy can be an environment-friendly Air Conditioner.
38. A mechanism for converting the solar heat energy into the mechanical energy could be very useful.

Attaining ideal state

"What is an ideal state?" I asked.

He replied, "There is a very old saying 'nothing is perfect'. Or nothing is permanent. Anyone who comes has to go someday. It is not only true for humans or animals, or living things but also for the things we use, the methods we use or the combination of different things we use to satisfy our specific needs. If we look at the past we can see how true it is.

Humans always strive to improve, to come up with something better to serve their needs, be it a better way to do things, an improved formula, an invention or innovation, or even better food to eat. We try to come up with ways to make things happen in the best possible way. We want to improve our surroundings and the environment and do something good for our society. We strive to ease our life, improve the quality of living, and make our life worth living.

It does not matter how small the thing is, how little contribution it will have in anything, product, solution, etc. It may be as small as a needle, remember, it is not going to be permanent. There will be changes, improvements, and new things coming up to replace the old ones. It is certain that after some time it has to be changed for good. Some things last longer, while others move out of existence soon.

Attaining an ideal state means you are making things better. Our elders tell us that nothing is perfect. And things always keep changing. So nothing can be termed as permanent but the sole nature of its own. Getting an ideal state means making things better than they were when we received them so that they can serve us better.

We can't say if something gives us exactly what we want, it is ideal. For example, we use television but is it perfect? Although it may seem so, but no, it's not perfect. Aren't there changes to it ever now and then? It always keeps updating – sometimes the picture quality, sometimes the sound, the technology, more and more sensors are added to give us a better experience, more and more features are added to it every day, it's getting thinner and thinner. Every new improvement looks perfect, more than we could ask for, but then again, there turns up something new, something better, something unique, something revolutionary. Perhaps one day you may find such a television which can make you feel everything so real, like the closest thing we have now is 3D televisions."

"How can you say that the products we are using today will be no longer be there after a few years or decades? I am wearing shirts, my father was also wearing shirts, my grandfather also used shirts and not only shirts there are lots of other things which are being used for so long time. I am unable to understand how we can say nothing lasts," I put forward my doubt.

He said, "Maybe your father and even his father wore shirts. But when you break the shirt into its component like the fibers, dye, methods of weaving, etc. which you are well aware being an engineering student, you would know how these have changed over the last few decades and even within a century. The shirt may have remained a shirt, but the kind of shirt, the kind of fiber, the methods of making and dying the shirt etc. have changed a lot. So the shirt you wear today is not the same as your father's or grandfather's. And it's not only about textiles, each and every field shows the same behavior. Change is inevitable.

Each and every product which is being used to serve the living beings on earth is going to be changed or modified, or newer products for same 'A' will come up within every five to ten years. In other words, every time interval of five to ten years brings in so many advancements in technologies, methods, thinking, etc. that are enough to change most of the products to the core."

"Having so many opportunities to bring in changes to just any product has made me confused. How should I decide which product I concentrate on to bring a change to it?" I asked.

He responded, "Well, you can do many things regarding this. You cannot choose any random product to work on. In future, you may get a better formula or solution than what I'm going to tell now. Discuss with your friends, what can be the possible changes in a particular product to improve it. Just do it for fun. You will love to do it if you have the right group of friends/students. But there is a problem about getting the right group. Try to be updated with the latest technologies, not only in the field you want to work but all, especially those which are even a little bit related to your field. Look for the product which has many problems. While doing so you may find any product you use very interesting. In fact, you may be able to find many such products, but try to focus on just a few. Look for the history of the product and the state of it which can be considered ideal. Look for its components. Again, go to the history of the components and look if the technologies involved need to be modified. It may take much time to decide what product should you concentrate on but once you are exploring the products in the above way, you will find the one you want to work on soon."

"Why every idea for the betterment of a product is not possible to be introduced in it for everyone?" I asked.

He drew a diagram and explained, "There is a **threshold for making an idea commercial.**

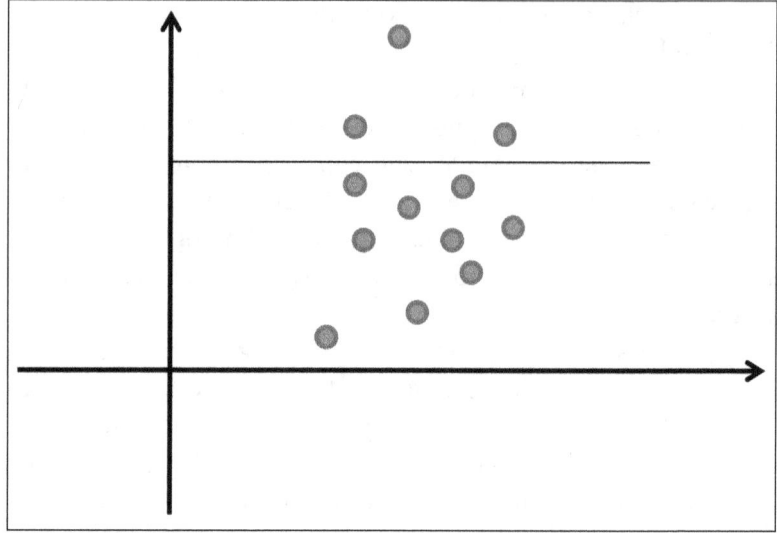

The line given above in the graph shows the threshold line for ideas qualified for a successful business. This success is time bounded and valid for a particular time period.

People have lots of ideas, many of which are good and get a great feedback. Based on that they also may receive some good contributions to bring their ideas into an ideal state. But it is not necessary that they all can be transformed into a business. Being good, having a good feedback, as well as the right backing is not always sufficient.

The line of the threshold is not fixed or same for everyone but is shifted according to the individuals, technology, time, place, and various other parameters. There are many other factors on which this line depends. What can be done by one person may not be done by another. Things that were not possible ten years ago are possible now. So, this line will keep moving accordingly.

If you are a student with many ideas, you will realize that some of them are not possible to turn into a good business maybe because of money, knowledge, time, risk, or other constraints. Many students have good ideas but they do not know where to start. Mostly they end up not working on the ideas. While those who get success in business, get it anyway, it doesn't matter even if the task they chose required very less money. "

"I think there are much more things other than products which need to reach an ideal state. So, why have you mentioned only about products to me?" I asked.

"Yes indeed. Only the products are not those which are changed to bring them to an ideal state, other things change too. Be patient, I'm coming to that and I'll tell you about the types of ideal state:

1. Time interval ideal state.
2. Product ideal state.
3. Process ideal state.
4. Service ideal state.

Time interval ideal state

In the time interval ideal state you take a time period required to do a certain task/activity and then you try to optimize it and bring it to its best, that is, bring it to its ideal state. For example, assume, it takes five days to do something and you aim to bring it down to two days or one day or even just a few hours.

Product ideal state

I have already told you much about the product ideal state. There would be thousands or millions of products, even related to the textiles. So, you have a big opportunity ahead of you. You come across just a few products in your daily life so you have less knowledge about the whole catalog of products that are available in the world. As much knowledge you gain in textiles, the products, the more problems you will be able to solve related to them even if you are not fully confronted by them. Similarly, you may have lesser knowledge about the industrial products, or some other fields, and their problems, which you don't come across in your daily life, but understanding the products, you may come up with a better solution for them as well. Thus, you should always try to gain knowledge and know more and more about products; this will increase your chances of getting to 'A'.

Process ideal state

It is quite similar to the product ideal state. Every process is aimed at making things easier. In this, although there are fewer opportunities and they are generally complex, process ideal state is easier to take place when we make changes to the product. The basic aim is to bring the process to an ideal state so that the end result can be achieved as quickly as possible and with better efficiency and quality with minimum faults or defects.

Service ideal state

We use so many services every day. Even the services can be modified and optimized to bring them to an optimized state or the ideal state. For example, many customers of a phone company are having the same query and they keep calling the customer care for that. Instead of a person sitting there listening to the same question again and again, and answering it to the customers, as the query is same, an automated machine can keep answering the question. Even better, if that is a general doubt, the phone company can send SMS notification to all its customers so that they don't have to call. Many of these things are done by the telecommunication companies, but this is just an example how a service can be optimized.

Now, I'm going to tell you more about opportunities related to theories

Particular theory opportunity

When you have a particular theory in mind you start exploring the possibilities of innovation and invention in that. When you say you want to work on nanotechnology, you actually mean you wish to explore the theory of this technology and work on it to bring about some good. Once you start working, you refine your work to your limited interest area which could be:

1. A single theory.
2. An assembled theory (i.e. a mixture of multiple theories).
3. A product opportunity in that field.
4. A product combined with theory.
5. A product combined with theory and modification.

Single theory: In this, you have only one theory that is main or the center of the application. For example, you may be able to find out a new application with the theory $E=mc^2$. You need to choose one theory on which the whole of your work will be based.

Assembled theory: In this, you have an opportunity to combine two or more theories, assemble them and use them for your application. These constitute the characteristics of both or all the theories and together they bring about probably more advanced forms of applications.

Product opportunity: Here we look for a product and then the opportunities we have to derive uses or applications through it. The more uses or applications we can find for the same product, the more useful it could be for the people and bring the product to an ideal state. For example, printers were initially used just for printing black and white documents. Slowly, printers turned into colored printers and they could print colored documents as well. And now, there are digital printers which can even be used to print on T-shirts, mugs, etc., and can even be used as scanners or photocopiers.

Product combined with theory: Here the application of a product is combined with a single theory or an assembled theory to bring about an outstanding solution.

Product combined with theory and modification: Here the application of a product is combined with a single or assembled theory and some modifications are made to it to arrive at an optimal and useful solution for the betterment of people or making their lives easier," he explained.

Problem specified incomplete opportunities

"If I have seen further it is by standing on the shoulder of giants."

—Isaac Newton

"What are the problems that some opportunities never complete?" I asked.

"Some opportunities remain incomplete even after great efforts have been put by the effort-maker. There are lots of people who try to accomplish and get a solution for their 'A' but some are unable to finish them successfully. If one is unsuccessful does not mean that the 'A' was wrong but it shows that maybe he/she did not try enough, and did not look in the right direction to get a solution. It could be that the effort wasn't sufficient, or it could be that something more was required than mere effort.

Every individual has some amount of 'B' to complete 'A' but that does not mean that person will necessarily be able to complete it. It depends on various things. There may be lots of projects in which nearly 90% of the required 'B' is available but the unavailability of that 10% can make the whole thing unsuccessful.

Task $\xrightarrow{\text{Brainstorming}}$ completed/not completed

Not complete $\xrightarrow{\text{More brainstorming}}$ completed/not completed

Not complete $\xrightarrow{\text{Additional things}}$ completed

There are millions of people who try to innovate, few of them complete, some sadly even die with their idea.

'A' $\xrightarrow{\text{Me}}$ Not Solved

'A' $\xrightarrow{\text{Me + other person}}$ solved

After graduation in 1792, Eli Whitney decided to leave New England and head south to fulfill his monetary needs. He did not know that within seven months of this decision, America would never be the same again. He had no idea what profound effect his decision could have on the history of America. Like others in the college, he had given a thought to becoming a lawyer, but fate had something else in store for him.

When he was employed by Catherine Greene in the South, he was asked to search for a solution which could separate the sticky green seeds from the fluffy white cotton bolls. The current process needed huge efforts and was time-consuming leading to almost no profits. It took him just a few months to come up with cotton gin. This was very useful because it could be used for small or large productions. For small productions, there was the smaller version of the gin which could be hand-cranked. For larger productions, a larger version of cotton gin was used which used water power and could be attached to a horse.

In 1888, a scientist named Friedrich Reinitzer was working at the University of Prague. He was faced with quite a strange phenomenon. He was a chemist and was trying to figure out the correct molecular formula for cholesterol. During experiments, he was trying to determine the melting point of this substance and found that it had two melting points 145.5 degree Celsius and 178.5 degree Celsius. It melted at 145.5 into a cloudy liquid, and at 178.5 the cloudiness vanished. Amid these temperatures was a state between liquid and solid. This concept was challenged by the scientific community where many other ideas came as answers to this question. Although Friedrich Reinitzer could not apply his discovery of liquid crystal then but later, in 1960, it attracted the physicist Pierre-Gilles de Gennes, working on superconductors and magnetic materials, to find a fascinating relation between liquid crystal and superconductors.

Again Pierre-Gilles de Gennes did his best throughout his life but no great inventions came within his time. During the later phases of the nineteenth century and the early twentieth century, the modern development of liquid crystal for application came into place and all the science behind it was deeply inspired by the work of Pierre-Gilles de Gennes," he said.

"But isn't the major problem - where to find these opportunities?" I asked.

He went on to explain, "Here are some of the ways through which you can chase opportunities:

1. People around us
2. Professors
3. Researchers
4. Companies
5. People of the past
6. Experiments
7. Articles

People around us

There are lots of people around, whom we see or meet every day - our colleagues, friends, ordinary people, poor people, etc. Knowingly or unknowingly they give lots of hints to have a topic for innovation. It may be a single person or many people who lead us to our topic of innovation. The number of people has no relation with getting the idea. Even a discussion among the students can lead to a breakthrough in that field. In the business world, it is generally considered that a group of four students can actually make a million dollar company. There are even investors who are ready to support such ambitious and creative students. In the same way, a group of students can lead to great inventions or innovations.

Only knowing the problems is not important, even an illiterate person can listen and tell his problems. The important thing is to filter the information and process it to reframe the problem in such a way that gives it a potential to become solvable. Thereon, you'll need lots of efforts and guts to go beyond the convention, face the traditional obstacles, myths, and statements, due to which the problems have not been solved till now and solve them. So, the next time, don't miss an opportunity to listen to the problems of your elders, colleagues, friends, etc. All these are opportunities for you, pointing you towards your 'A'.

Professors

Even today, consulting professors is the most widely used methods to get an 'A' in any field for inventions, discovery, etc. Professors generally have lots of 'B' and experience and can give good pointers towards a meaningful 'A'. Most of the noble laureates got their 'A' by their professors/mentors.

Researchers

Researchers are those who know and have explored lots of things in their arena. But you should refer to lots of researchers so that you can find diversity in the ideas. This diversity may give you another area to explore.

Thomas Edison's bulb was the first application of vacuum tubes. After discovery, he placed a third electrode to see what effect it brings on the 'cathode rays'. These were made of electrons which he had named as 'corpuscles'. Edison tried his best and did whatever was possible.

Joseph John Thomson developed a vacuum tube to investigate the cathode rays. He later found that what Edison had named as 'corpuscles' was a particle which is found in most materials.

Companies

Companies have problems mostly related to manufacturing, service, etc. Companies can conformably tell you how important a task is i.e. they already have the conformity of a solution of 'A' in the market. Now what they need is to solve the problems related to it. For example, if there is a company which has a problem statement to design a better coffee machine, you can chase that to make a better coffee machine with a new design, because the company already conforms to the demand for these, the market is already there, you don't need to create a market for your product.

People of the past

Lots of people have died with their ideas only in the books written on their works. The people who come under this category are scientists, novelists, philosophers, etc. You need to go through the books based on them to see just how many of them had such great ideas which never materialized late until after them. Analyze to see what all is there in those books and see what needs or needed to be refined to make that idea work. Thereon, pull up your socks and get on with solving the issues. You don't need to go 100 or 200 years back. You may even look up the unfinished works from someone who maybe just passed last year.

Experiments

Experiments are something which reveal and validate lots of information in some specific areas. These revelations and information can lead to various solutions and ideas which can turn into inventions and innovations.

Articles

There are lots of chances to get information from articles, and this information may not be complete or may have scope for improvements. The articles can also point to ideas and problems which need to be solved. So as discussed before, articles/passages are a great way to explore the fields and find 'A'.

Required

"What is meant by the term 'required'?" I asked. "If anything which has not been made before but is needed by anyone, be it an individual person, corporate organization, government organization, college, university, research organization, etc., is termed as a required product/application. It is something in which the requirement is there but the product has not yet been created. It doesn't matter if the product can be made in the current time or not, the first and most important step is to have the requirement. Required applications/products are predefined innovative goods. A requirement can be as simple as an analysis for someone on some imaginary parameters.

As the end product is the result of pre-defined requirements, the configurations also need to be dictated beforehand. This forecasting is done keeping in mind its feasibility under the given conditions. The configuration is based on some assumptions to remove the pain points which the analyst or the researcher can foresee or think of, once he/she has understood the requirements. Fulfilling the requirements and factoring the optimal configurations, the newly made product is most likely to bring things to a better level.

For example, any production company always has a requirement of betterment in production. It is a continuous process. There are lots of flaws that exist in any company which need to be resolved or removed. At times, some solutions are provided to remove some flaws but they may introduce some new ones. Also, the product and development companies are always under pressure to bring products which can win the hearts of the users.

They all need some 'required applications/products' which not always can be made in-house or by their own employees. These can even be identified and provided by doing some modifications to the existing products or solutions and may be done by experts in the field, ordinary people, or even students. It doesn't matter who provides the solution, these companies are looking for someone who can come and solve their problems.

These required applications/products may not always be actually required by themselves. At times, they foresee an opportunity of growth through certain applications and products, and hence they want them to be made. They always have to strive for progress and such applications/products could be their gateway to it. Some companies which do not focus on innovations or keeping themselves up to the mark, generally see a downfall. Their need to people keeps on decreasing and they themselves keep degrading, resulting in their complete wipeout. Each company needs a vision and a mission to give them a broader 'A' and keep them going. That is why they always align themselves with that single goal in which they strive to be the experts or market leaders. These companies are focused on customers and keep their promises in mind. They sustain through constant delivery keeping themselves industrially updated, adopting the latest technologies and technological changes. They do not indulge in being rigid about forcing outdated concepts, technologies or products on customers to fulfill their own ego.

In the 19th century, people knew whoever is able to invent a good sewing machine could become rich. Inspired by this requirement, Issac Singer and Elias Howe were the first men to become amazingly wealthy from their invention of sewing machines," he said.

"So you are basically saying that if I can find any required application and work on that, and if I am able to come out with a solution then it may bring a huge benefit for those who required it as well as for me. It seems to be like a win-win situation," I said.

He replied, "You can say so, but chances of a win-win are when you get to find the required application through others rather than yourself, that is, something which is really needed by someone else, then be it people, company, college, organization, etc. Your own requirement or required application/product may not be that commercially needed. Here, I'll tell you ways to explore the required applications/products/solution to problems optimally:

Facts related to problems

Unknown problems	No problems	Known problems
• Visionaries (G)	• You (A) • Professionals (C) • Classmates (D) • Visionaries (G)	• You (A) • Neighbours (B) • Professionals (C) • Classmates (D) • Company (E) personnel • Workers (F) • Visionaries (G)

Company

• G	• A • E • G • C	• A • B • C • D • E • F • G

College

- G

- A
- E
- G
- C

- A
- B
- C
- D
- E
- F
- G

Organisation

- G

- A
- E
- G
- C

- A
- B
- C
- D
- E
- F
- G

Research Org.

- G

- A
- E
- G
- C

- A
- B
- C
- D
- E
- F
- G

Individual

- G

- A
- E
- G
- C

- A
- B
- C
- D
- E
- F
- G

Entrepreneur

- G

- A
- E
- G
- C

- A
- B
- C
- D
- E
- F
- G

Branching of problems

"What are these known problems, unknown problems, and no problems? I am not able to understand," I asked.

"Quite simple. Actually, these are the types of problems. When I say known problems, it means even the common people know about these. For example, when a machine stops working then everybody knows that there is some problem.

When there is a problem which common people don't even see it as a problem then it is called no problem. For example, when a farmer works too hard for his field he takes it for granted that he has to work hard and there is no way he could make it easier for himself. He just does not see that this could be sorted in some way. He doesn't seek help or go to any technical person to sort out his problems because he doesn't even acknowledge it.

In the same way, when the most advanced, learned or technical people don't think that there is a problem which exists in the current scenario that is called an unknown problem. For example, during experiments, even the most skilled person may stumble with the results and may not see the result as a problem while only a few experts can tell that there is some problem."

"What are the places where applications are required?" I asked.

He answered, "The requirement of applications can be at various places:

1. Colleges
2. Companies
3. Research organizations
4. Individuals
5. Entrepreneurs

This list is not exhaustive and these are only a few places where applications may be required. The types of requirements may vary but there could be many more places where applications may be needed.

Usually, the firm/organization which has the need for an application doesn't have much idea about its solution. Nearly every organization has some required application for which they are willing to seek a solution but they may not be capable by themselves to build it in-house. So, they rely on others'/external help. It happens occasionally that people who are filled with knowledge do not get the problem to solve and the people with a lot of problems do not have enough knowledge or willingness to solve them. As we see, there are two parties involved in this – one that finds a problem or gives a requirement, and the other which tries to provide a solution. These arenas to bring in or suggest a response or a solution may not be open to all. Especially bigger organizations tend to hire other technically expert and skilled companies or experts to help them with solutions. If an in-house solution is attained and is acceptable then it's ok, else the problem or requirement is handed over to others to solve. If no solution is arrived at and the problem statement or requirement remains unfulfilled even by the experts it is considered as a non-solvable problem.

College and required application

The colleges have some very different type of required applications. They may be related to their own problems or student's problems. These problems may be that of college policies or that of some new machinery which may fulfill most of its requirements. Overall, the required applications in a college may be quite less to give much opportunity to most enthusiasts trying to find out their 'A' and come up with some innovations, hence, it's not advisable to concentrate all your energy on trying to find out the required applications for a college.

Students may have quite a few required applications related to their project work or practical assignments. So, through these required applications you may have a broad opportunity to come up with some useful/meaningful/helpful things. As students have a very dynamic mind and they process quite a lot information, so they do need certain applications to fulfill their needs.

The number of required applications may vary but it is certain that every college does need some applications. Most innovative colleges are expected to have more required applications.

Companies and required application

Companies have a broad array of required applications. They can require applications starting from very small projects to the very large ones which may even require a whole new concept to renovate their business. These are very necessary for their growth. Every company makes some small in-house projects or prototypes of their required applications. They are clear about what exactly they want. Generally, a research and development department of a company does this job. There are many companies which keep themselves updated and keep innovating. They stay ahead of time as well as needs and hence, remain unbeatable making them the market leaders. In today's world, to keep innovating is quite necessary for survival.

Research organizations

Not only the research organizations, where lots of experiments take place, but any place where experiments happen or if there is a group of people who think of something innovative then you can get an idea for a required application. The invention of vacuum tube triode helped push the development of computers. In the late 1940's the limitation of these tubes was reached. As more and more computers were made, newer designs were proposed to improve them. But to achieve those designs, more number of triodes were required and the circuits became quite complex. As a solution engineers packed several triodes into one vacuum tube to make the tube circuits simpler and more efficient. Soon they found the flaws in doing this - the vacuum tubes tended to leak and the metal emitting the electrons got burned out. The tubes also needed quite a lot of energy to run. These problems collated as a requirement, the solution of which resulted in the invention of semiconductors."

Section-3

Processing of 'A'

"Now you've got your 'A' and by doing so you have overcome one of the biggest hurdles in your way. How is this 'A' going to help you depends on how much experience you gained while selecting and processing 'A'. Whatever I have told you till now will take you far ahead of most people who are still struggling to find 'A'. I'll explain you the 'ABCD' formula or rule in detail, which I mentioned before," he said.

"Oh yes! You discussed this briefly one day, but I'd like to hear more about it," I said excitedly.

He continued, "Whatever you decide as 'A', it's very important to know how to handle it, otherwise it may consume a lot of your time and effort and soon you may be leaving it aside. The time taken to get to a solution is dependent on various factors but it is quite necessary to know what can be handled, what cannot be handled and how to have a grip on what cannot be handled.

Once you decide 'A', there are a lot of things that will come to your mind - The first and the foremost is 'A', another is the timeline to get a solution for it. Besides these, there are countless problems which may pop up and make you feel of leaving the idea and live your life peacefully. Hence, this time period/timeline must be reduced to the minimum so that you can do lots of things in that short span of time, and not lose interest in the idea resulting in dropping it completely. If you go through the history, you'll find that scientists or people who dedicated themselves to some 'A' took many years to come out with their concepts in practical form.

Having an idea is one thing and working on it is another. It's like - Having a life is a fortunate thing to happen but living it well is another thing. The method given in this book is based on how your mind works and thinks. We think of having ideas and working on them day and night. But the solution of working day and night may not work if:

1. You feel that the idea is not so worthy.
2. You think you are not smart enough to continue.
3. You think experts would have already tried this, so why I should waste my time on it.

So it becomes quite important that you choose something to which you can give your full heart.

The science decades ago was not so accurate that it could give 100% results but today, it has become quite advanced and the results are pretty much accurate. We humans are getting better day by day. Some people do not go in depth to study complete results and then end up inferring that the world is at its downfall. They say the past was much better than today. The method is kept as simple as possible along with its complexity which increases with time and the need of an idea. You can handle a complex thing if you have a strong base and are properly motivated to dedicate your best efforts with excitement and eagerness towards it. In this method both these parameters increase simultaneously. Hence, there is a better possibility for you to arrive at a solution, and you would know the problem and solution very well."

"Are there any types of 'A'?" I asked.

He replied, "As I discussed in my initial discussion, 'A' is a topic having many possibilities or types. Refer to the diagram I showed earlier. The aim of working on 'A' or solving 'A' is to bring some betterment which may occur by solving a problem, through innovation or invention, a quest towards an idea, etc. It is something which once achieved also gives one a better state of mind to the one who achieves it. You may be confused how a problem may be equal to an idea or a statement or an expression etc. but when you think deeply you will find that ultimately they all are the same = requirement. These are all possibilities of 'A' or types of 'A' and depend on what one decides to work on ultimately, or how one sees the requirement. In terms of the users, one may not clearly define if the requirement is a problem, an idea, a statement etc. It can vary and all depends upon the solver how he/she sees it and wants to solve it. The possibilities or types of 'A', from the diagram I showed you earlier, are as follows:

1. Problems
2. Ideas
3. Requirements
4. Statements
5. Products
6. Thinking
7. Analysis

These are only a few ways to look at 'A' but these can be different according to the innovator. These can even be expressions, imaginations, facts, etc. Classifying 'A' will help you decide what you are going to do.

For example, you may arrive at an 'A' which is: cooling of a building with water as it is quite cheap in certain areas especially if the city/building is near a large water body like the sea, river, lake, etc. You can also arrive at 'A' through the following ways:

Looking at the problem: You may concentrate on the problem of the building getting hot and the conventional methods to cool it down are quite expensive.

An idea while brainstorming: While brainstorming, you may get an idea of cooling down the building by using the specific heat of water.

Inspired by a statement: You may be inspired by making a statement that how much energy is required to cool down the building. Your calculation may bring you to the statement 'if we could insulate a building and install a vein of water throughout the building then it may be possible to maintain a lower temperature.'

Although the 'A' you arrive at through various ways may seem different at first but if you look closely, in all of the above scenarios, 'A' is the same. Howsoever you may arrive at your 'A', the ultimate goal (to make things better) remains the same, now you may call it as a problem, a requirement, an idea, a statement or whatever, it's up to you. Basically, you will be working on something to improve the quality of your life.

Various examples of 'A' could be:

1. Cooling of a room through drop splitter.
2. Improved children bicycle with an automatic control system.
3. Re-dye-able garments.
4. Air conditioned chair.

"In order to get a solution for 'A', can I keep my thinking as it is or do I have to change it?" I asked.

Robin replied, "Well, it can work either way. But in case you wish to stick to your thinking, you may modify 'A' to match it. You can do this in the following ways:

Modification of 'A'

When a raw, unpolished idea comes to our mind we refine it to avoid any clashes with our thinking. Having a precise 'A' makes it easily understandable to us as well as others. A not so precise 'A' may even cause confusions and hinder our way of working towards a solution, so one should always try to be precise. There is no way to make 'A' ideally correct but there are certain treatments which can make it precise.

Don't keep a wide/broad scope of 'A' unless necessary: When you define 'A', try to be as specific as possible. Try not to let it have a huge/wide scope that it may deviate from its initial purpose and lose its way. Keep it limited, keep it to the point, and keep it accurate. For example, you may have an idea to make the education system better through technology. You got an idea to define your 'A' which is: an improvement in the education system. This 'A' is not very clear and accurate. It has a wide scope and does not tell exactly what improvement you are talking about or how you want to bring the improvement. To make it clear you could put it as: 'improvement in the education system through technology for faster access to knowledge.'

Change it if you think it could be made better: You should very well change your 'A' whenever you think it can be put in a better way or you think that you have better ideas to do the things you had thought of initially. For example, once I thought of 'making the room cool through the cooling effect of drop splitter' – that was my 'A'. But soon I realized I could put it in a more accurate way so I redefined it to – 'closed environment cooling through the cooling effect of drop splitter.' The solution of 'A' would be applicable to any closed environment and not just limited merely to a room. It gives a clearer picture and thought process.

Examples:-

1. Planning, analyzing, designing, and estimation of the natural cooling tower.
   Modified from: Bringing the natural cooling tower to a better state.
2. Civil project on soil stabilization and reinforcement.
   Modified from: Bringing soil stabilization to its ideal state.
3. The design of elevated service reservoir.
   Modified from: A better design for elevated service reservoir.
4. Analysis and execution of road construction work on NH-5.
   Modified form: Better road construction.
5. Analysis and design of the multi-storied residential building.
   Modified form: better multi-storied residential building.
6. Microscopic modeling of pedestrian dynamics.
   Modified form: theory of pedestrian dynamics (microscopic).

"Alright. I got a good picture about 'A'. Could you please elaborate on 'B' now? I asked.

'B' and types of 'B'

'B' is almost synonymous with knowledge. It helps us get things done faster. Our mind is built to process things for which some prior knowledge is necessary. So, it has a direct relation to the knowledge which we gain through various resources. The resources may be in the form of books, articles, videos, newspaper, audio etc. Books are the most common while the rest of the sources of knowledge are becoming very popular and relevant these days. The Internet is the fastest growing and latest way to gain knowledge.

Now you may wonder why there is a necessity of listing 'B' or having it available somewhere. It is required for the following reasons:

1. To check the authenticity of your knowledge whenever required.
2. To know how much you have progressed with respect to your work.
3. To know what more you need to understand.
4. To get the knowledge again whenever they are required.

Types of 'B'

1. Books
2. Articles
3. Videos
4. Audios
5. Internet

Just like to stay healthy, eating food is important, feeding the mind is equally important.

Whatever you know today is a result of feeding your mind with knowledge and experience. To get significant results with quality from your mind, you'll need to feed it with lots of meaningful information. Unlike the ancient times where knowledge was the privilege of a chosen few, we are lucky to have been born in an age where knowledge is available in abundance and there is almost no restriction to what you want to learn and know. In fact, the available knowledge would me much more than an average human can know completely in one lifetime.

Importance of time while selecting 'B'

The time factor is important to keep oneself motivated. So, you should know well how much time your selected 'B' may take to bring you to a level of solving the problem. The more accurately you can calculate this, the better it is. Sometimes you may feel that it may take endless time to gain this knowledge which may be demotivating and you may end up giving up on your idea or 'A'. So it's vital to judge an approximate time beforehand.

Also remember, don't get too attached to 'B'. Knowledge is quite necessary but it is not 'everything' that you need to solve 'A'. Getting attached to 'B' you may end up spending way more time than you thought of studying the materials and things which may not even be related to 'A' or help you solve your problem.

I think you have got sufficient information on 'B' now, so let me move on to 'C' and its types.

'C' and its types

'C' is something which we conclude after going through 'B'. These conclusions can be of three types.

1. Continuous type (C1).
2. Semi-continuous type (C2).
3. Random 'C' (C3).

C1 (Continuous C)

The continuous 'C' or 'C1' is synonymous to unceasing conclusions and tracking of the status of your work. Here you make a list of all your activities and keep updating the status of your work and where you stand. This especially becomes important when you have multiple ideas. You keep putting in the highs and lows of the project, and your feelings (good as well as bad) about it along with any ideas which you think can affect the project, in a broad way. A correlation between the ideas and feelings is not a must.

I have seen many people talk about the technical challenges with much curiosity one day and leaving the idea another day. They don't differentiate between the regular feelings and notions they have about a particular idea and the actual technical challenges. If you have a big expectation from an idea and you haven't achieved that, you have two opposite feelings related to that one feeling - one which makes you feel positive while the other makes you feel the opposite. This feeling kills your creativity and most people leave their ideas because of it. It's similar to the feeling when you do public speaking for the first time and feel embarrassed. You'll notice each and every activity you do and think about feels so weird and makes butterflies run about in your stomach. In the same way, you look upon your ideas and compare them with your limited perception making you feel how weird they are.

If you brainstormed throughout the day but couldn't come out with any reasonably positive solution or direction, you are bound to not feel comfortable and start getting ideas which may be out of desperation and not be good for your original ideas.

Reason behind writing 'C1'

1. It will be hard for you to know the status of your idea and its possibility of success if you look at it after a gap, later.
2. It will help you predict the major problems well in time even before you have invested too much time on it.

3. To know about the consequences of the reaction of your mind to an idea.
4. It is a path to get ideas.
5. Getting the block which is stopping you from going ahead.

For example, if your mind says you don't have enough knowledge to solve the problem you either go ahead and search what knowledge your mind says you need to go ahead and go on if you're able to make it then, or you pause your work till you get sufficient knowledge but you mention why you stopped from working further.

C2 (Semi-continuous)

It is the most productive brainstorming of an idea. After going through 'B' we get more ideas related to a topic. Every idea has a series of ideas, problems, solutions, benefits, drawback etc. and these come one after the other. We may get an idea followed by a problem then by another idea followed by a solution of the earlier generated problem and so on. It is the core of brainstorming.

C3 (Random C)

These are the random thoughts that can occur after attaining 'B' and may or may not be directly related to your idea or topic but must be noted down as they can be useful then or later in one way or another. These are generally productive inferences from the knowledge attained which help solve or avoid many problems while working on your idea.

'D' and type of 'D'

'D' is closely synonymous to 'A' and makes a good contribution to make your 'A' clearer, crisp, and accurate. You can deduce 'D' from 'B' and 'C'. Just like 'A', 'D' may be

1. An idea
2. Product

151

3. Principle
4. Theory
5. Assumption
6. Statement

'D' can any of the above or a combination of them.

'D' in an idea

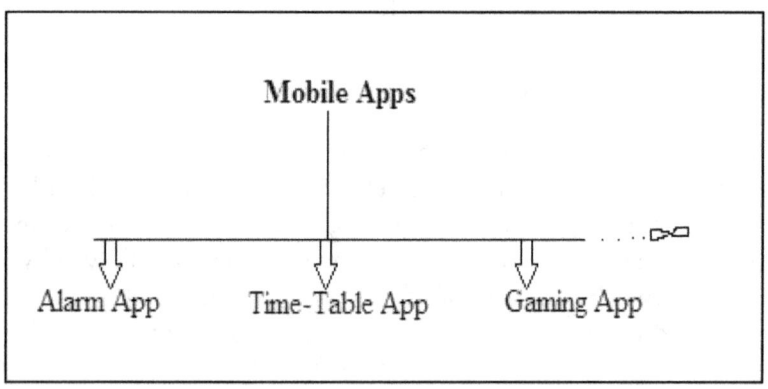

Alarm app: Let's say an individual is willing to make a very useful app for the students. He analyses and finds that getting up in the morning or at any time of the day could be really challenging. So he/she gets an idea to make such an alarm which, like the conventional alarms, does wake up the user but without causing any discomfort or agony to him/her. He/she is thinking about creating a sizeable app which uses the concepts of philosophy and the behavior and mental state of an individual to provide a pleasant waking experience to its users.

Timetable app: Suppose a person thinks about a timetable app which provides various choices and flexibilities. For example, the timetable may start with studying of half an hour at first and after completing that one may have an option to go on further e.g. one hour, two hours etc., or pause there itself.

'D' in a product

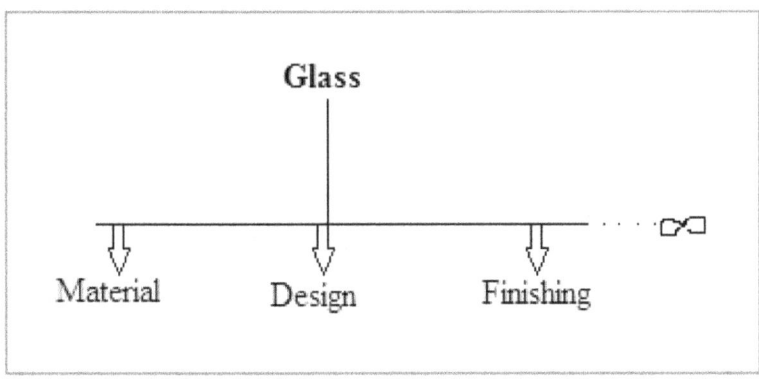

While having a product you have to assemble its parts to get the real product which exists. So, you may have to put together the 'D' which are related to each other. Here, an example of a glass has been given to you and you may have to find the parts/ components of the glass which make it complete.

'D' in principle

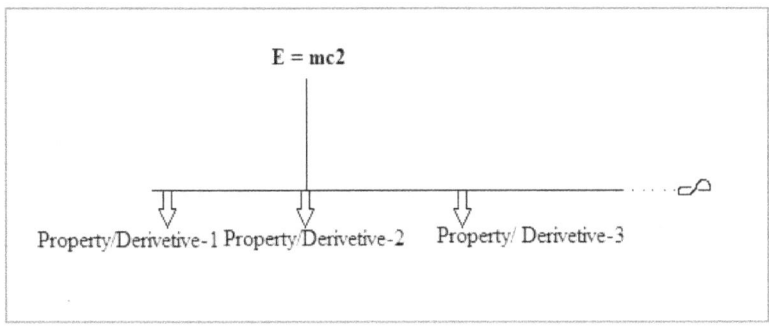

Already having a principle or a formula, you just have to put the properties of it as 'D'.

'D' in assumptions

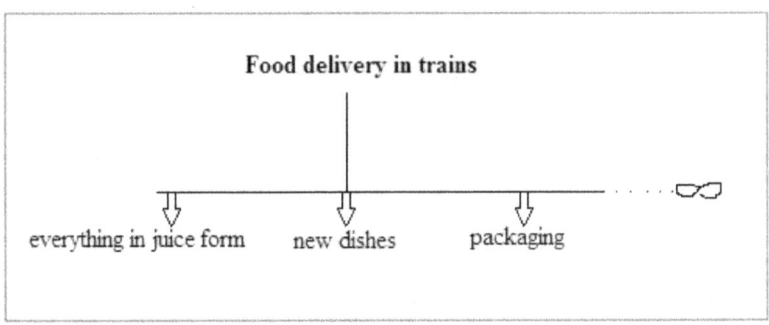

Here the topic of 'A' is food and its delivery. The food delivery needs to be made in trains. 'D' may be based on our assumptions and pre-conceived notions about the food and its delivery mechanism in trains.

'D' in statements

The various components of 'A' can be understood through the example below, combining which we arrive at 'D'."

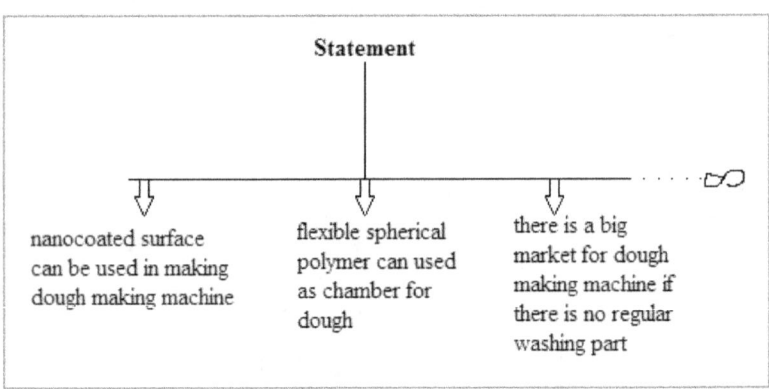

Now that I've given an idea about 'A', 'B', 'C' and 'D', I think it's time to put them together and understand the ABCD formula as a whole."

"I am really excited," I said.

ABCD Formula

This formula starts with an 'A'. Once you have your 'A', you try and gain as much knowledge and do as much research as you can ('B') to find a solution to it. Thereon, based on this 'B' you come to certain meaningful conclusions ('C') leading you to a more accurate and refined form of your starting point, called 'D'. This 'D' can simply be seen as a richer/purer 'A' on which you may start doing the whole process again, i.e. gaining further knowledge or doing more research whatever is required ('B'), coming out with fresh conclusions ('C') based on 'B' and getting a polished 'D'. 'D' remains 'D' until you start working on it. Once you start working on 'D', it becomes your new 'A'.

If you look closely, the ABCD formula follows a cyclic pattern. This rule seems like a network because that's how our mind thinks. Our thoughts are mostly connected somewhere to the previous thoughts. In fact, some of the thoughts are caused by the immediately preceding thoughts, while some others come into the mind due to some old thoughts.

Our thoughts are also connected to the information we pass on to our mind. We read books, watch videos, or even when we look at our surroundings, our mind starts generating thoughts.

Whatever 'A' you have, there will be some 'B' related to it. Some of the 'B' will be already existing, while some of it may be required to be defined through your research and analysis. You focus on the 'B' which you think will be related to your 'A'. Different people have different sets of 'B' and they all can be right. Collecting 'B' is an art which may take some time to surface and be understood.

In every ABCD the 'D' gives a better explanation to the initial 'A'. Each iteration gives you a better, more refined, and accurate 'A' and brings you closer to the solution.

You have 'A' and 'B' in addition to your own thinking. All these combine together to result in 'C', the conclusion/conclusions derived from 'B'.

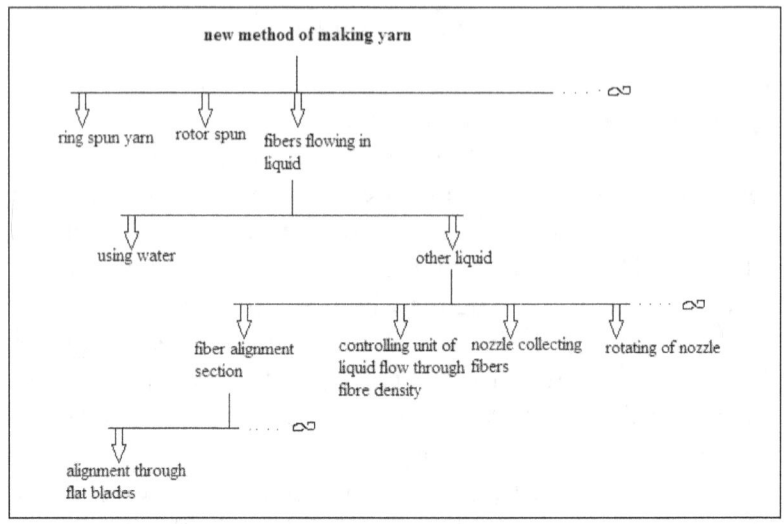

From the above diagram, you can see that the complete picture does not come out while thinking for the first time. With each conclusion and brainstorming session, you move a step ahead, and there are so many iterations and steps you go through before reaching the final one. You may think 'I am going to invent a new method of making yarn. But how to proceed?' Soon you start believing that no method to create yarn is perfect so you move forward and start thinking about a new method of fiber interlacement. You feel that if it is possible to reduce the numerous steps of the process of making yarn then it could be helpful. You start thinking about making yarn with the least number of steps. You may first think of plucking yarn from the bale of fibers. On brainstorming, you realize that it may not be successful as this may restrict the behavior of yarn and the fiber may get entangled easily. So you may finally think of using water, which in turn you generalize to some liquids having more appropriate properties than water and could be more suitable than it.

You can see this stepwise as follows:

You list down all ideas or ways you can improve the yarn making method. You pick each, brainstorm over them and zero in on one of the methods, 'fibers flowing in liquid' in this case. Now, you start thinking on the next level. If you have more ideas to make the yarn you write those in parallel, otherwise you will proceed in the series.

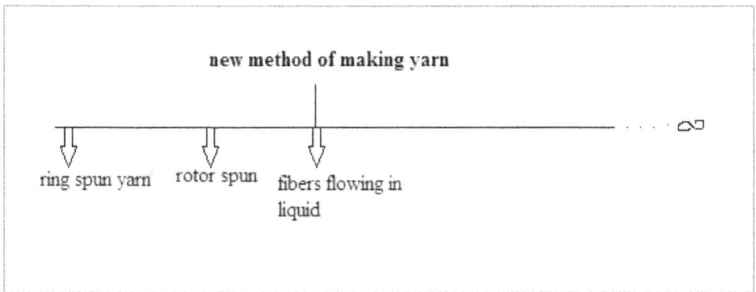

After the above thinking you may get the next one of using water or some other suitable liquid:

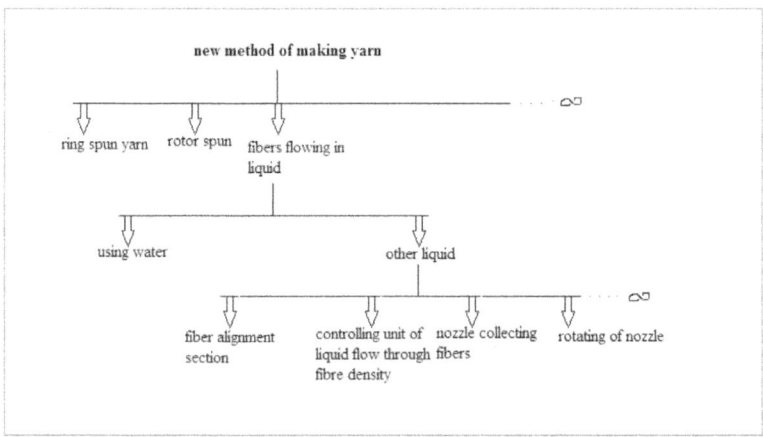

This is just a sample of the thought process in mind. Here the details of 'B' and 'C' have not been given and you will notice that the whole ABCD chart is not complete yet. Once you are committedly working and brainstorming over this, you'll be able to write the 'B' and 'C' as well.

157

How to start with ABCD

You can start with ABCD as you wish. But you may be a little confused about the starting point. For avoiding this confusion I'll give you a certain way through which you can make things easy.

To work using the ABCD formula, you start by making ABCD charts. The first time when you are making the ABCD chart, start with 'A' and then jot down all the existing solutions for your 'A' and add all the new methods/solutions you can think of (we'll keep these as 'D' as we'll be actually brainstorming and working on one of these). For example:

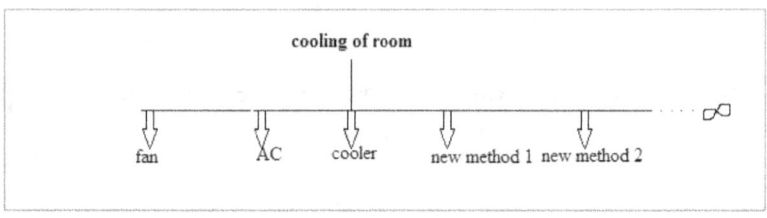

These are just examples and you may include any number of existing solutions. Noting down the existing solutions is important because it may help you compare the existing methods with the new methods you have in your mind. You can also depict the above diagram in the following way:

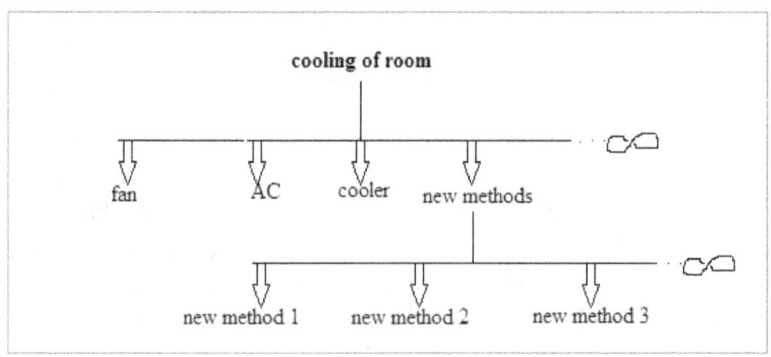

Types of ABCD based on transition

1. Temporary ABCD.
2. Permanent ABCD.
3. Better ABCD.

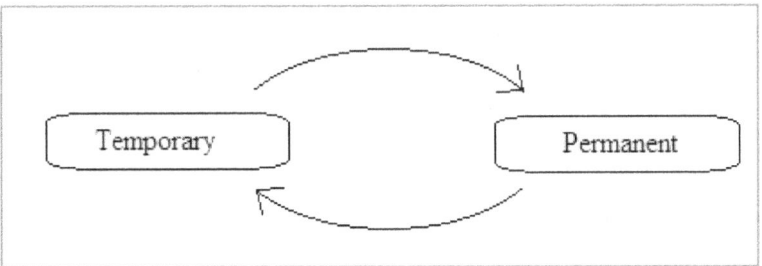

We get ideas which can be represented in the form of ABCD. Probably thousands of these come and go in our mind daily. Sometimes they swing in and out so fast that we don't even acknowledge them. Some of them you notice very brightly but most of them are left and forgotten. These are temporary ABCD.

The permanent ABCD are those which remain with us for a longer time and we tend to work on them to solve problems.

The temporary and permanent are swappable. It's just like we meet lots of people daily in our life but we don't get acquainted with each and every one. Some of them are just come and go, while some others stick around. But even those who you know well may not stay with you for long. Similarly, there is a chance of permanent ABCD to become temporary and leave.

Next is the better ABCD chart. Here you change the whole ABCD chart with a new one. You do it because of following reasons:

1. The previous chart is not turning out to make things better.
2. You wish to think on the same topic but in a completely different ways.
3. Bringing change to the existing chart is tough.

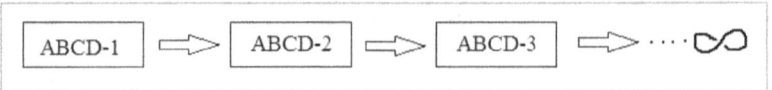

The above diagram shows many ABCDs for the same/similar 'A'. You are not advised to have a 'better ABCD chart' with more than five ABCDs for the same/similar 'A' simultaneously. It will eat away your time. Remember that transforming to a better chart is good and you may do that multiple times but having more than five ABCDs in the above chart will not help. If such a situation arises then try to merge them and bring them down to a maximum of five.

Types of ABCD based on ABCD chain

1. Single ABCD.
2. Multiple ABCD.

In single ABCD there is only one thought chain that comes to your mind and you can easily put that down on paper. It looks as below:

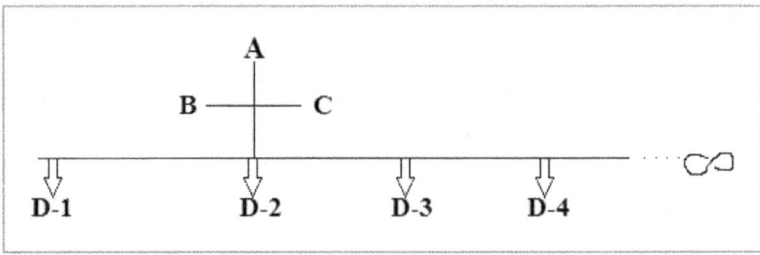

In multiple ABCD there is a more complex thought process and you are weighing your options and thinking about ways in different directions. So, it will have more than one chain. This happens quite often and looks as below:

160

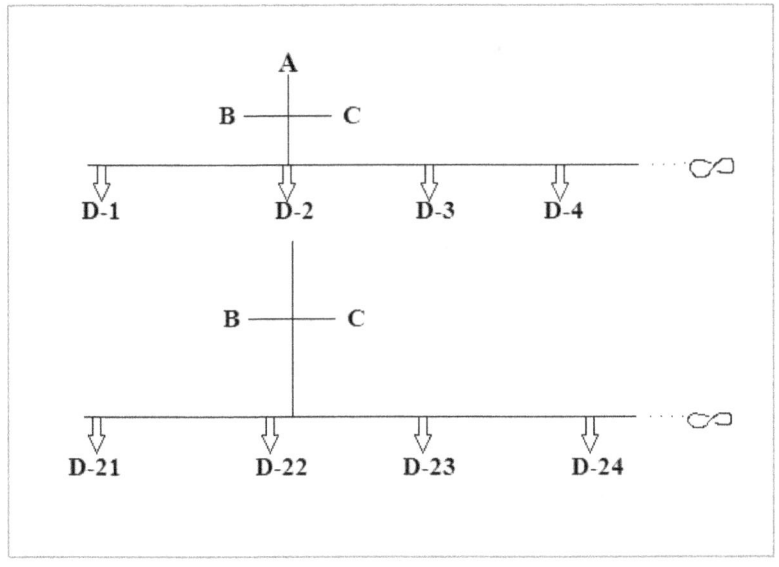

Types of ABCD based on 'A' and 'D'

1. Real A imaginary D.
2. Real D imaginary A.
3. Real A real D.
4. Imaginary A imaginary D.
5. Real A and real and imaginary D.

* * *

Now, I have given you sufficient knowledge to progress on the path of innovation. This knowledge may not be exhaustive but is sufficient. Below I'll give you some examples. Remember, these may not be absolute but are some things that scientists have faced and you will come to know about lots of things through these.

Examples

In this section, I will give you a few examples on how some inventors invented products that changed the world. I'll start with the invention of Blue LED which took a lot of time and effort. In 2014 Isamu Akasaki, Hiroshi Amano, and Shuji Nakamura received Nobel Prize in physics for the invention of efficient blue light-emitting diodes which has enabled bright and energy-saving white light sources.

I am going to tell you about the problems faced by Isamu Akasaki. When he started working on this topic there were already many scientists who were trying to innovate the Blue LED. There was a huge possibility that seeing so many scientists working on the problem already and watching many fail, he could have abstained from working on it, but he took a chance and decided to work on it. There were many materials which were a strong candidate for the Blue LED. This is how he explored and picked up Gallium Nitride for the research.

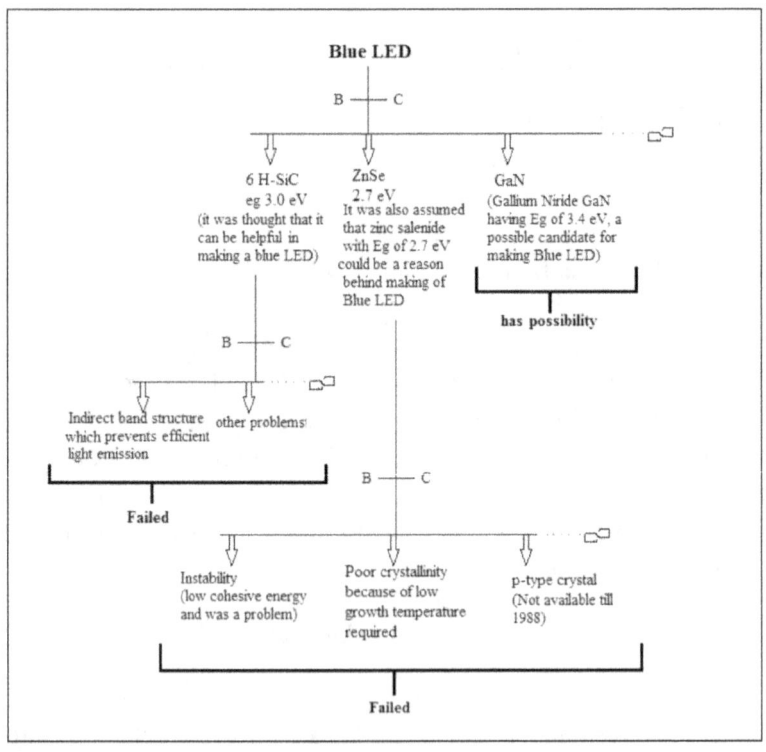

After concentrating on GaN he, along with his team, started looking for the manufacturing methods of it. They thought of making the p-type and n-type components which are very important to make LEDs. But the materials are not always in those forms in which you require. First knowing that any

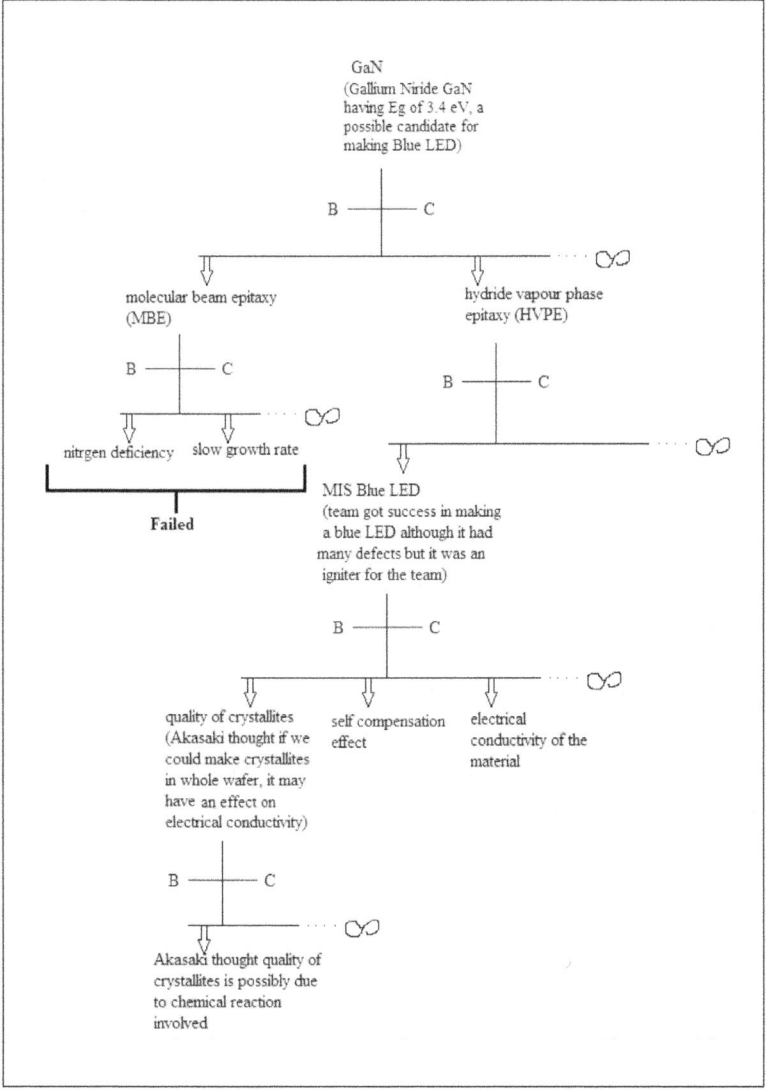

improvement can be a solution, is, in itself a big task. Then getting the solution of the problem is another. By the method of HVPE, the team got a success in making an MIS type LED. But this LED had a very low efficiency (0.12%). For the whole world it may not be a big step but for them, it was like a drop of water for someone dying of thirst. He knew it was a breakthrough. Thereon, they focused themselves on improving the quality of GaN through the chemical reactions involved.

Now they faced a new challenge. They had to find such a method which had the possibility to make GaN having the property they required. They not only tried different methods but also they invented some. One method which worked for them was called metalorganic chemical vapor deposition (MOCVD).

Finally, his team got success in getting a very high-quality GaN. It was not the end of the problems because they were yet to make the p-type and n-type GaN. You may think, 'I just missed a chance of inventing the Blue LED. If Isamu Akasaki, Suzi Nakamura, and Hiroshi Amano had not invented it then I would have been the one to invent it.' We read stories of invention and think how easy it was getting the solution. We think so because we know the answer and how it was arrived at, now. If I tell you 'Graphene has lots of qualities and has a big market. If someone could find a method of manufacturing it cheaply, it will be a big leap in the field of nanotechnology', you would face a major dilemma - whether a method can really be found if you go chasing it. They too would have felt the same when they started.

Next, I'm going to tell you about Arunachalam Muruganantham, who invented a cheap manufacturing process for sanitary napkins. He just got an idea of it when he analyzed his wife using a dirty cloth for the purpose.

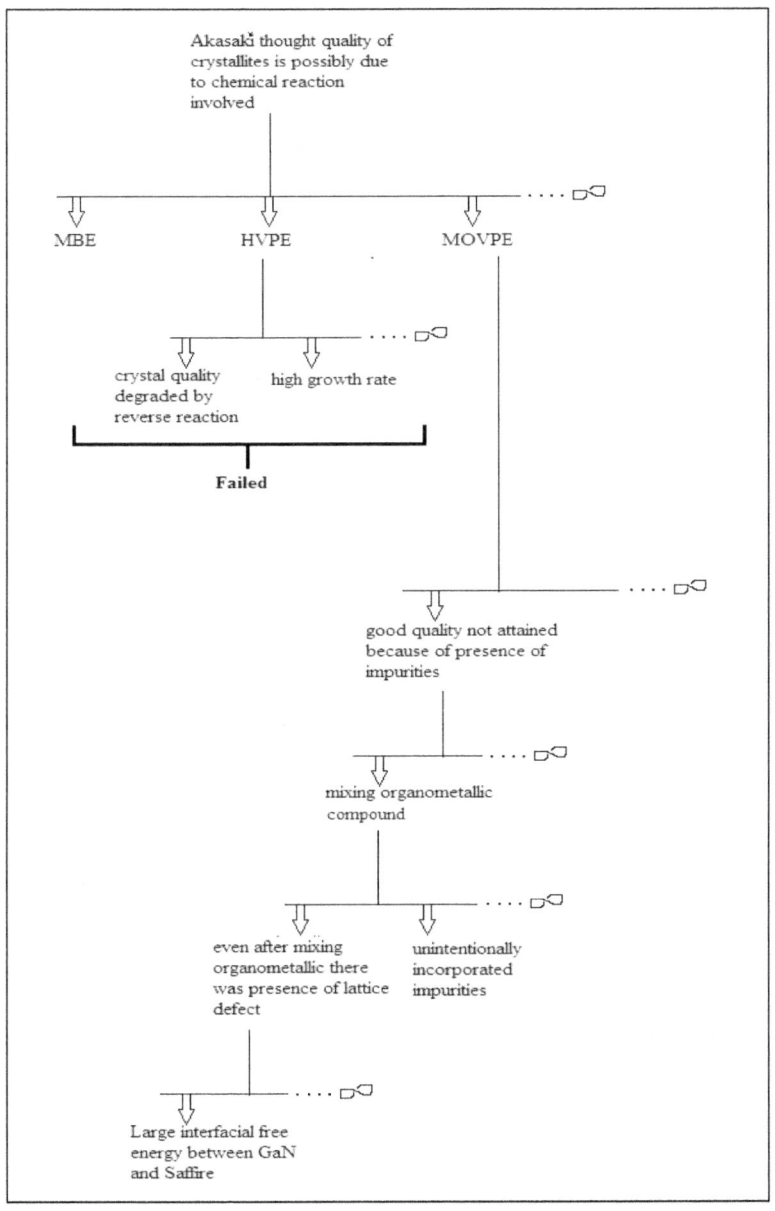

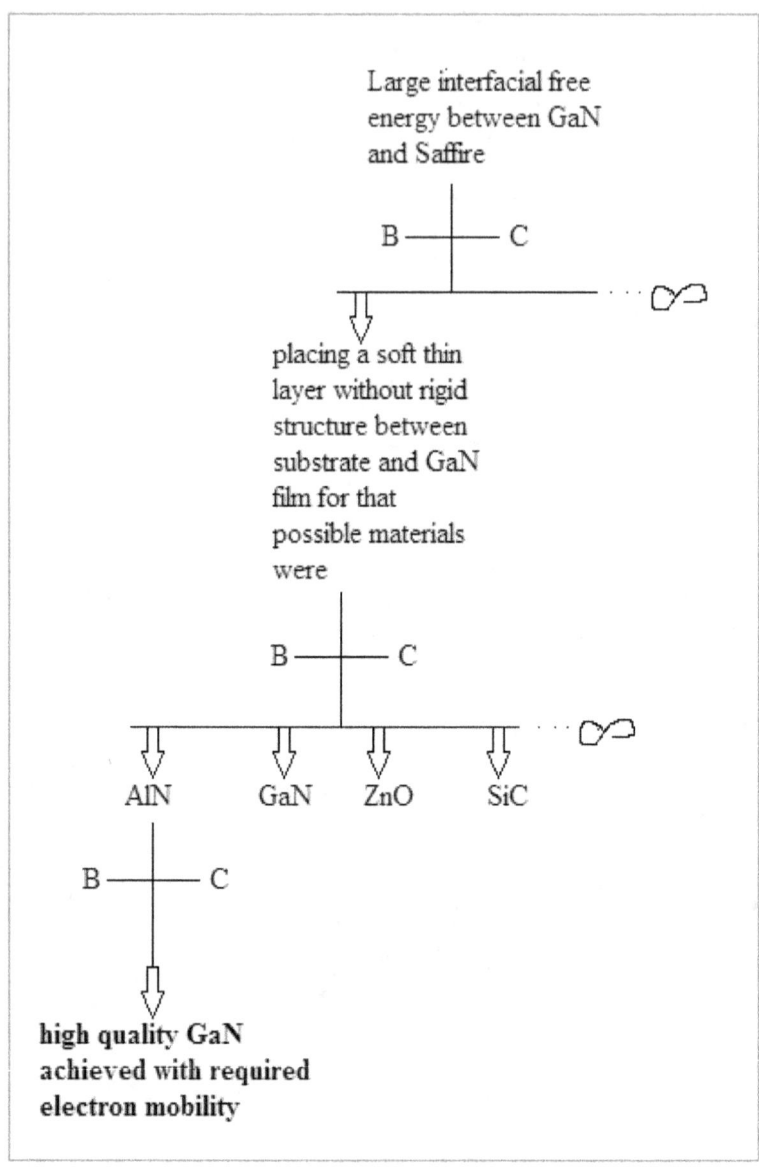

For us, this story may be laughable but for him, all these were hurdles on his path. You can brainstorm easily but when you actually start performing experiments or doing the practical,

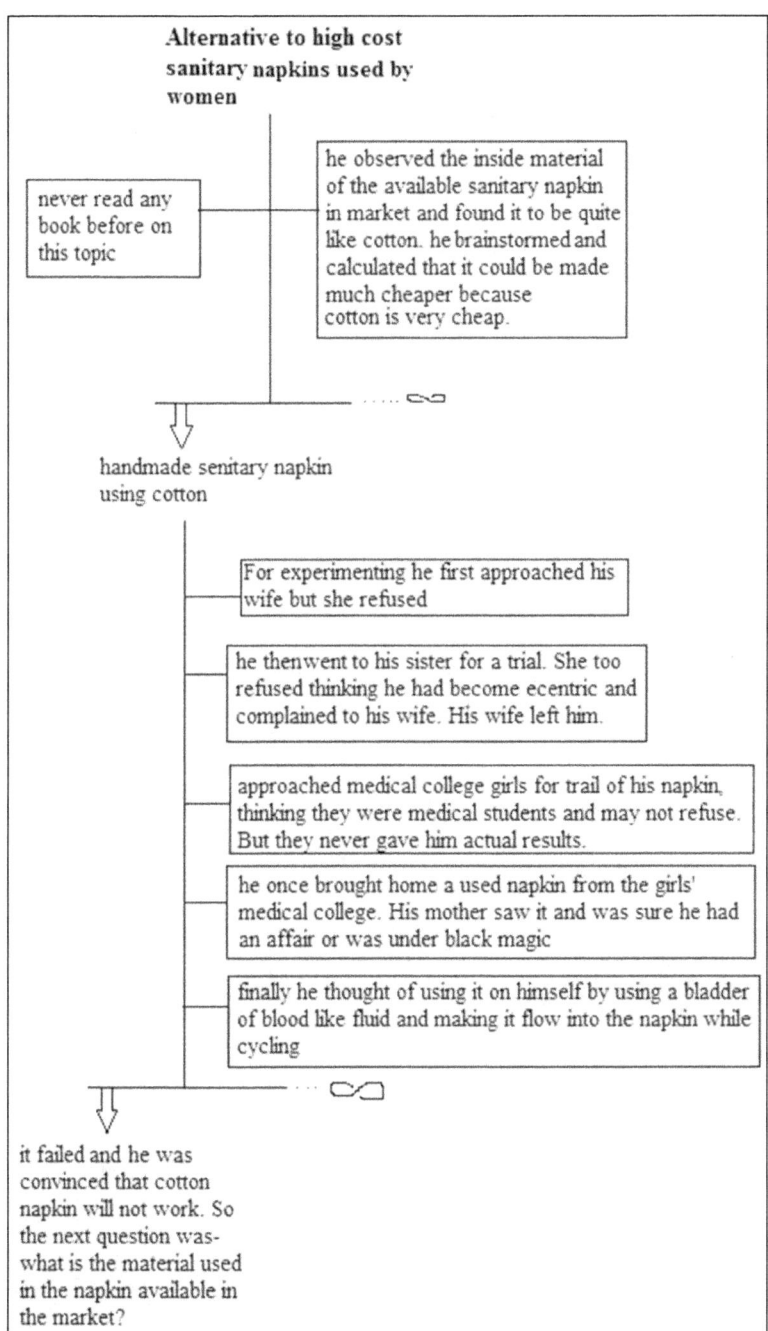

Alternative to high cost
sanitary napkins used by
women

never read any
book before on
this topic

he observed the inside material
of the available sanitary napkin
in market and found it to be quite
like cotton. he brainstormed and
calculated that it could be made
much cheaper because
cotton is very cheap.

handmade senitary napkin
using cotton

For experimenting he first approached his
wife but she refused

he then went to his sister for a trial. She too
refused thinking he had become ecentric and
complained to his wife. His wife left him.

approached medical college girls for trail of his napkin,
thinking they were medical students and may not refuse.
But they never gave him actual results.

he once brought home a used napkin from the girls'
medical college. His mother saw it and was sure he had
an affair or was under black magic

finally he thought of using it on himself by using a bladder
of blood like fluid and making it flow into the napkin while
cycling

it failed and he was
convinced that cotton
napkin will not work. So
the next question was-
what is the material used
in the napkin available in
the market?

167

the problems increase many folds. You need to find methods which are low in cost but give substantial outcomes.

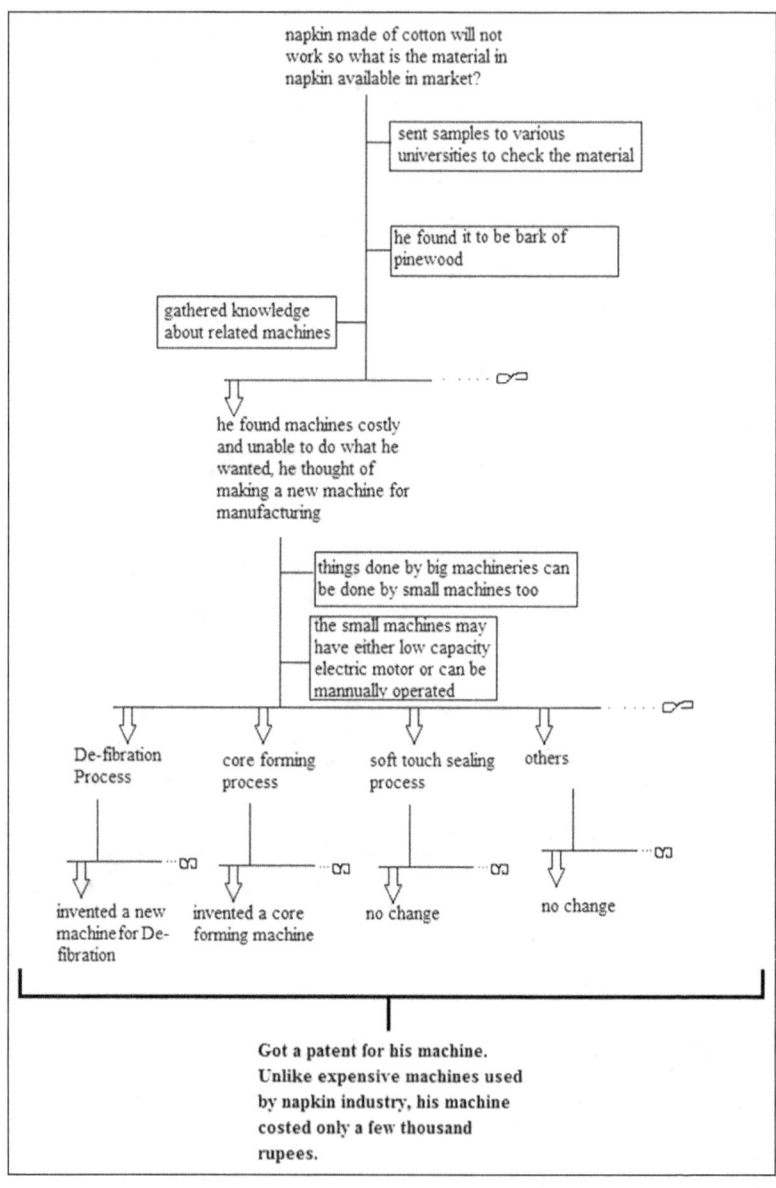

You see how he got success in creating a manufacturing machine when initially he had no knowledge about fibers, manufacturing processes, etc. All he had was an idea, a problem at hand, on which he focused dedicatedly and came out with a solution.

* * *

"It's been quite a long time since I have been coming here, I think almost a year," said Robin.

"Maybe, but I don't think so. It seems just like yesterday," I said reminding him of the first day we met at the garden.

"I have to go to the Bangalore headquarters tomorrow. After that I shall head to another country within a week," he said.

"So early? Why didn't you tell me before and what about our remaining discussions?" I asked.

"What I have taught you is sufficient. Now it's your time to explore. Whatever I have told you is my life long experience. I'm sure you will reap some benefit from it. I have documented it in detail. But tell me one thing, what difference do you see in your attitude before you met me and now?" he asked.

"A lot of changes. Not only in the attitude towards myself but also in the attitude of observing things. I don't have words to explain it but it has brought me to the next level of confidence. The fear which I endured for so long has gone now. I feel a kind of freedom. The freedom is inspiring me to do something more instead of just thinking about the pros and cons which I always do. Also, now I can imagine how any invention, innovation, and research can be done. Before I met you, I used to think that innovative people are those talented ones having a mindset quite different from the average people like me. A sense of 'doing' is driving me now."

"Good. So I guess it means I have something worthy for the students," he smiled.

"Not only worthy. It's 'super worthy'. It seems like you have explained the science behind innovation, invention, and how our mind works," I said.

"That may not be accurate but somewhat close. What do you say?" he asked.

"Yes sure, slowly it is reaching the ideal state of explanation," I said with a smile. He was packing up and I was thinking what more quality talk we can have.

Before I could think of anything he said, "I can see a bright future in your eyes," and left me filled with a great sense of self-confidence.

* * *

It's been six months since he left the city and me. I miss him very much. Every day, getting something new was such an enriching experience and made my day interesting. I got a boost in my daily activities. If you are internally confident, everything goes in the right direction and smoothly. I started working on various ideas. I engaged myself with the college on the project of 'Air conditioned mattresses and 'cooling through drop splitting effect'. I did quite well and managed to file a patent, the review of which is currently in progress. With only a few days of college remaining, I started working on a new and innovative idea - 'recycling textiles'. I'll tell you how I arrived at this idea.

Just like many passages which Robin gave me, here is the one I took seriously and got this idea.

Textile recycling innovation challenges clothing industry

There are many methods to recycle the textile products. Textile recycling is the process through which the rejected clothing and other textile materials are recovered for reuse or recovering of the material. Usually, the textile recycling involves donation, collection, sorting, and processing. The global textile industry has evolved into a $1 trillion business. Over 80 billion garments are produced annually. It is worth noting that the rate of textile recovery is still only 15%. While natural fibers consume a lot of time, space, labor, water, electricity, etc. resources, many of *which are rendered useless just after a few uses, synthetic fibers have are not designed for recycling and are harmful to the environment while in production as well as when decomposed. If the qualities of clothing are good, they are sorted and categorized by color, size, and quality. After that, they are prepared in the form of bales. A bale is a compressed form, which is easy to transport and takes less space for storage. The process not only creates jobs but also the apparel can be used again giving more value for the money and resources spent. The only drawback of this method to reuse the apparel is that the value of the apparel, along with the shine and luster of the fabric decreases. Once the color of the fabric fades it does not seem attractive. In another method of recycling the fibers are recovered from the materials and then converted into industrial wiping cloths and other items.*

If the material is made of synthetic then they are recycled in a different manner, in fact, they are never used as is. First, they are filtered to remove the unwanted materials like buttons or metallic components. Then they are recycled into polymer chips. These polymer chips are again used to make fibers or other materials.

In India, the recycling of textile material is a little bit different. There are small scale industries to work on the second hand imported clothing and create a wide range of products. The products may be yarn, blankets, doormats, mattresses, and bed linen. Some pieces of cloth are cut down in square and rectangle piece and they are used in making home cleaning and industrial wipes.

As there are a variety of fibers so the recycling practice is different. Cotton, wool, acrylic, polyester, silk, nylon etc. are the most common fibers. For recycling of wool and acrylic waste, Panipat the world's largest textile recycling hub produces 'shoddy' wool yarn from used winter clothing. They are produced in yarns, blanket, felt products. The business of using recycled acrylic and woolen threads for blanket manufacturing has annual revenues of up to 1000 crores in Panipat alone.

The recycling of textiles has great potential for innovation and creating more value from the fibers. Most recycled textile materials last only the first recycling. The second, third, and more stages of recycling hardly take place. Many apparels can be recycled to the same material even for the second and third recycling.

At first, I went through this passage and it made me think about the topic. Then I went through many similar passages and related videos on the internet. As I was going through these, many solutions started coming to my mind.

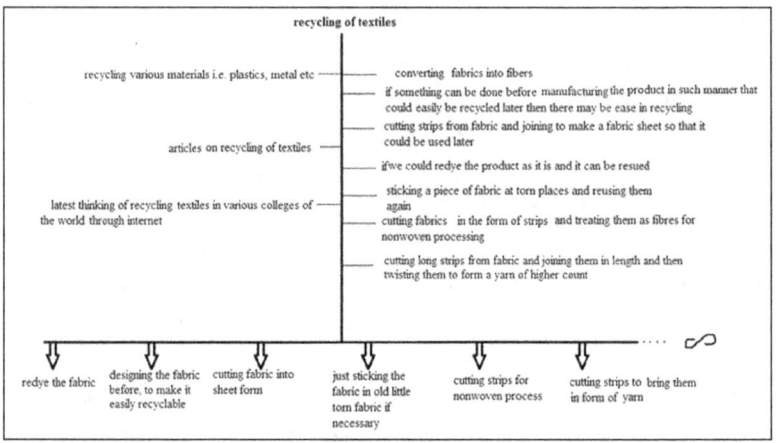

Re-dyeing the fabric is - when you get a fresh fabric and are bored of using it, you want to change it. How can you do that? You re-dye it and make it ready for reuse. The solution provided here does not work for torn fabrics or apparels.

An apparel could be designed in such a way that it could help recycling. Although, I don't even know how it would be possible, but it's an idea, it's a start.

The concept of cutting the strips of fabric has come in many times, so you can make a better ABCD by thinking of merging these strips into one apparel. Each strip is different from the other. Strips are cut in the form of squares or rectangles and then joined together whether by sewing or any other suitable methods.

To make yarn from the cut strips concept you can cut the fabric in the form of long strips (a few millimeters to several centimeters) and then join them with any of the methods, followed by twisting them together.

I tried to merge re-dyeing and redesigning of the fabric and apparel. I thought of redesigning because if the apparel was torn from some critical place then it needs to be changed in such a way that it doesn't look like a rectification. For example, mostly trousers tear from the bottom edges near the heels. So, if we could design that portion separately, which, with today's technologically advanced machines doesn't look like a challenge, then it may increase the life cycle of the trousers. For shirts, the collar and elbow are the most critical parts where redesigning may help ease their recycling and increase their life. Although, there may be a challenge of making them good looking and defect free.

THE END

www.ingramcontent.com/pod-product-compliance
Lightning Source LLC
Chambersburg PA
CBHW071302220526
45468CB00001B/246